DARK VOICES

To John

Great to meet you in Malvoques
at the Myths of Voice Festival 2005

Yours vocally

Noah

Roy Hart in *L'Economiste*, April 1975.

DARK VOICES

The Genesis of Roy Hart Theatre
VOLUME I

NOAH PIKES

with a new preface and foreword by
Jay Livernois

Spring Journal Books
New Orleans, Louisiana

Africa Series 1

Published by
Spring Journal, Inc.;
627 Ursulines Street;
New Orleans, Louisiana 70116

Printed in Canada.
Text printed on acidfree paper.

Edited by C. L. Sebrell and JFL.

Cover design by Christopher Ludwig.

The cover image is of
Roy Hart rehearsing *Ich Bin*
from a photograph by Ivan Midderigh in 1973,
used with his kind permission.

Library in Congress Cataloging in Publication Data

Pikes, Noah.
    Dark voices : the genesis of Roy Hart Theatre / Noah Pikes ;
with a foreword by Jay Livernois.
        v. cm. -- (Africa series ; 1)
    ISBN 1-882670-19-1
        1. Roy Hart Theatre (Theater group) 2. Hart, Roy, 1926-75 3. Pikes, Noah. I. Title. II.
    Africa series (Woodstock, Conn.) ; 1.

PN2639.5.T54 P55 2000
792'.09421--dc21

                                                                    00-057339

This revised edition is dedicated to my wife, Annabeth Mühlemann.

Alfred Wolfsohn and Marita Günther in a singing lesson, 1956.

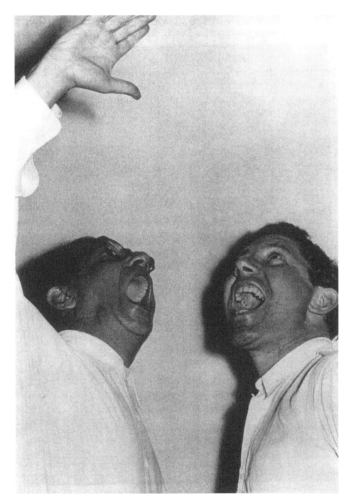

Alfred Wolfsohn and Roy Hart in a singing lesson, 1955.

Contents

Acknowledgments

First, it is essential that I acknowledge the fact that this book is a personal account of events, ideas, experiences, and stories to which many individuals over decades have contributed. Their accounts would be different to mine. However, this is not simply an autobiography as I have called upon the testimony of a considerable number of other people because the nature of the story I have to tell is too multifaceted to come only from my memory. Still, I know that the choices I have made in the use of their generous contributions are my own. This book is also augmented by numerous quotations taken from material published in books, press, private correspondence, and where necessary, permission to do so was received before its inclusion.

So, I would like to go to those who have made this book possible. The nature of my debt to Roy Hart and Alfred Wolfsohn will become evident to the reader as an ongoing, interwoven thread. Here, I can only thank the *daimon* that led me to Roy Hart's door.

This book owes overriding thanks to Marita Günther for her care over several decades of the as yet unpublished manuscripts of Alfred Wolfsohn, for her dedicated work in translating them all into English, and for her permission to quote extensively from them. I would be delighted if this book brings Marita's long-held dream of their full publication to realisation. Gratitude to her, and to other colleagues from Roy Hart Theatre, Rossignol (Derek Rosen), Robert Harvey, and Kaya Anderson, whose written and spoken memories of the 40s and 50s gave me new temporal perspectives. Thanks is also due to Sheila Braggins whose memories of working with Wolfsohn are unique.

In addition to them, there are those whose recall began with the 60s and 70s, and their accounts were invaluable in giving substance, colour, and on many occasions, unknown details, to my own memories. They are Ian Magilton, (to whom extra thanks is owed for various word suggestions which have been integrated into the text and for which he is not directly attributed,) Paul Silber (who is a special contributor for his unique account of Roy Hart's death), Clara Silber, Kevin Crawford, Linda Wise, Enrique Pardo, Lisa Mayer, Pascale Ben, David Goldsworthy, Margaret Pikes, Saule Ryan, Jonathan Hart, Coco Samuels, Matthew Dunne, and Richard Armstrong, whose memory of moments and details was particularly vivid. Thanks too to Agnès Dumouchel, a former member of Roy Hart Theatre, for the use of several recorded interviews with members of the company she made in 1984. Similar thanks is extended to Appy Chandler for use of tapes which he made in 1995.

I would like to thank Derek Gale whose unique experience of both Wolfsohn's and Hart's legacies and his working contact with many members of Roy Hart Theatre in the 80s informed his support and creative proof reading. My appreciation for the corrections of many details go also to Saule Ryan, Margaret Pikes, Kaya Anderson, Marita Günther, and Sheila Braggins. My gratitude to Bertil Sylvander for his insistence that this book needs to be written, and whose voice will be heard in the sequel to this book.

Concerning the photographic material used, I would like to belatedly thank my departed parents for my baby picture. Authorship of photos from the Wolfsohn period is not clearly known, though Kaya Anderson is known to be the photographer of some of those from Wolfsohn's later years. Of those depicting events within the Roy Hart Theatre, where authorship is unstated, unless it came from a newspaper, it inevitably belongs to one of the five photographers active within the group itself during the 60s and 70s, viz. David Goldsworthy, Saule Ryan, Joseph Clarke, Ivan Midderigh, and Ian Magilton. Ivan Midderigh was responsible for the front cover photograph of Roy Hart in rehearsal of "Ich Bin," and thanks goes to him for his permission to use it.

I would like to extend my gratitude to James Hillman for the inspiration of his re-visioned psychology, and his creative doubts about the future of psycho-therapy; doubts which have opened up a space in which I believe the legacy of Hart and Wolfsohn naturally stand.

Thanks also for James Hillman's introduction to Dr. Helmut Barz. It was through Dr. Barz's support when he was the President of the Curatorium (Board of Governors) at the C. G. Jung Institute at Küsnacht, Switzerland, that I began to entertain the idea of this book. Dr. Barz also introduced me to the late Susan Bach, to whose Foundation and its Trustees I am most grateful for invaluable financial support at several stages of this book. Although well into her eighties when we met, Susan Bach's astute mind and concern for relevant and coherent writing were the major reason for a reorientation in my approach that led to my first published writing, the article "Giving Voice to Hell," in *Spring* 55.

An unique kind of gratitude goes to my publisher, Jay Livernois, who never wavered from his immediately affirmative, "Yes!" when I first enquired if Spring Journal Books might possibly be interested in publishing this story. His counsel has extended to levels beyond simply that of business. Warm thanks also to the editor, C. L. Sebrell, for casting her spell over many of the more meandering passages and bringing order to them.

Gratitude to Annabeth Mühlemann, my wife, for her ongoing and loving support in so many delicate ways.

I give my thanks to Philippa Cornforth and William Horder for their generous hospitality in London during the early stages of my working on this project. And thank you Harold Pinter for allowing me to interview you about your meeting Roy Hart.

Thanks also goes to Sonu Shamdasani for pointing me in the direction of some-thing valuable that had been under my nose for many years in Zürich, and to my student and friend, Veronika Latini, for translating its meaning once it was located. This ex-change of letters between Alfred Wolfsohn and C.G. Jung is included as an appendix in this revised edition.

Thanks to my students, and to all those who have worked with Roy Hart Theatre and expressed a desire to know more about the background and history of its unique approach to voice. To them, especially, I would warn you against taking this book as a gospel and suggest treating it more as my gnostic way of responding to your continued interest and questions about the origins, ideas, and development of the work you yourselves have experienced in more recent times.

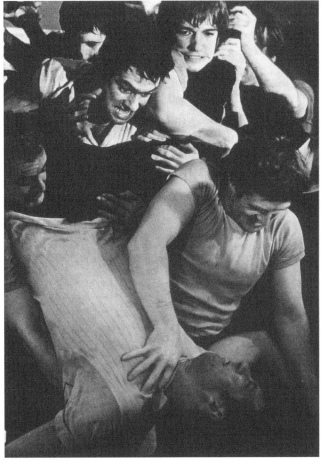

The death of Pentheus from *The Bacchae*, 1969.

New Preface

Richard Ellmann's 1983 revised edition of James Joyce's biography contained as many as five hundred and thirty-six text changes. This new revised edition of Noah Pikes' *Dark Voices* (volume one of the story of the Roy Hart Theatre), does not contain nearly a quarter as many. Still the errors, necessary changes, and refinements were numerous. And even one mistake in the first edition of a book leads to such anguish for writer, editor, and publisher, we wonder why write and publish ever, especially if the unintended consequence is to drown in the complexes brought about by the whole act. Although the answer to this problem probably is to just go out and have a good lunch and forget about it (a time honored tradition in publishing especially when those lunches included three martinis in Manhattan), over the last five years since the first edition of *Dark Voices* came out, we have had time and put in the effort to improve the work and correct many of the mistakes found. So with this revised edition, we hope to confine the first edition to the role of a collector's item; a book to take a place in the list of *curiosa*.

Still, as previously stated, we have checked and rechecked every date and fact and quote. There have also been changes made to the text so that nuances of meaning and language have been sharpened to try to convey more closely what occurred or what was meant in the first edition but did not come out as desired. These changes, though, are dependent more upon a writerly fantasy than any literal fact as a history or biography seems to transform itself in its retelling, becoming more incredible than fiction due to its real nature.

However the most important change has not been a correction of date, name, place, typographical error, or subtlety. This new edition now includes parts of the correspondence of Alfred Wolfsohn and C. G. Jung. The excerpts from these letters show how the originator of much of the voice work used by the Roy Hart Theatre, Alfred Wolfsohn, felt that there was a tie which existed between his ideas and those of C. G. Jung. The letters between them express a desire on the part of Wolfsohn for a meeting and personal connection with Jung which never happened.

Yet there remains a mystery in this story of correspondence between Jung and Wolfsohn. Their first arranged meeting in Berlin in 1936 never happened, and Jung never allowed Wolfsohn to meet him in Switzerland before Wolfsohn emigrated to England. Did they not meet because of Jung's busy schedule or was there a wall set up because of Wolfsohn's Jewish background (and it was especially dangerous then to meet with a German Jew)? Or was it something else not yet found hidden in this history? Even now the Jung heirs will not release a copy of Wolfsohn's letter to Jung in 1937 (see the appendix) because of what they claim as "medical confidentiality" (Huh? Wolfsohn has been dead for more than forty years, and he had no children!).Well we leave the judgement and resolution of these questions up to you, the reader. After all mystery and ambiguity rarely hurt the pleasure of a good story, which, we hope you will agree, *Dark Voices* is.

Jay Livernois
Eranos, July 2004

Foreword

Noah Pikes is an odd and brilliant man who works with people and their voices. He calls the idea of this work "the Whole Voice." He believes that he works with the voice in the creative tensions found in dualities and their oppositions, specifically in the sounds and psychological resonances of body/soul, male/female, inner/outer, light/dark, up/down, good/evil. Yet Pikes' work did not originate with him. It is rooted in the vision and the discoveries of the German experimental voice teacher, Alfred Wolfsohn (and his pioneering theories which coalesced into what he called "the unchained human voice"), and the 60s avant-garde theater techniques of the English actor, Roy Hart. This book (and a subsequent volume) is the story of the genesis of these ideas.

Although the phrase, "the Whole Voice," can be anathema to some post-archetypalists, a scratch on its New Age sounding surface reveals that what Pikes is proposing is the development of a polyphony and not a wholeness. "The Whole Voice" does not and is not moving to a unity or harmony. On the contrary, what Pikes searches for through his techniques using "the Whole Voice" are the other dimensions of voice besides its usual expression in and through bland aesthetics. Instead he uses these other dimensions, let us say cracks, as a way into the imaginal and—here I hesitate to use the word due to its contemporary overuse—soul.

In past ancient cultures, particularly neolithic ones, the sound made by the name of a person, creature, or object was identified with its soul and was thought to carry power. To know a name was to have power over that person, creature, or thing named. This is why Metacomet, the seventeenth century New England Algonkian sachem, was known to the English colonists by their name for him, King Phillip, and not by his native American name. It was only after he was defeated and beheaded by English colonial Indian allies that his true name was revealed. Metacomet, being a traditionalist, had hid his name by allowing the New England colonists to call him Phillip (after Phillip of Macedon, while ironically his older brother was called Alexander) for fear that they would come to control his life soul, and he would lose his "Indianess."

Shamans are well known to use voice with its full range of sound making possibilities. Mircea Eliade tells us that the presence of animal spirits (gods) during a shamanic session is manifested by the imitation (by the shaman) of animal sounds, especially if the shaman is possessed by one of the spirits. "The language of the animals" is often the secret language of shamanism, because it is the voice of the gods which connects the shaman to the other world of divine beings.

"The Whole Voice," this voice that echoes shamans and ancient culture, is not pretty (nor is it simply shocking). It is disturbing as most things are that touch soul in our contemporary culture of studied mediocrity, whether a great lecture, being in love, raw conversation, a startling person, a pornographic book, or a delicious bottle of wine. This voice, from its simple practice to a full blown performance, can be divine.

I first had a glimpse of this divinity in a performance of Leoncavallo's *Pagliacci* given by actors from Roy Hart Theatre (Linda Wise, Ian Magilton, Jonathan Hart, and Rossignol) in Locarno, Switzerland in the summer of 1983 while attending the Eranos Conference in nearby Ascona. I was swept away by the performance and its use of voice and movement. The experience moved me to visit the Roy Hart Theatre Centre at Malérargues in the south of France that next winter.

Accompanied by Charles Boer (later joined by James Hillman and his analyst friend from Santa Fe), and unlike my reticent (although wickedly funny) friend, I jumped into the theater training that was going on at Malérargues in January 1984. I took voice classes (taught by Liza Mayer, Kevin Crawford, and privately, Rossignol), Kevin Crawford's dance classes, and Enrique Pardo's movement classes (where I first met Noah Pikes rolling on the floor among bamboo sticks). I even cut up a large pile of firewood for heating the chateau and its out-buildings (they make up the physical plant of the Centre). And at every chance I went out drinking with acting students from Italy, Holland, France, and Scandanavia (and especially with a tall, spike-haired blonde from Sweden).

While there, almost nightly performances were put on for us, although it sometimes seemed that we were the performance for the members of the Centre at Malérargues. Dinners were eaten (especially Pascale Ben's duck at the rented estate of Olivet), wine flowed, and lasting associations were made with performers. In the meantime, the voice work permeated and affected everyone, while the ideas and ghosts of Alfred Wolfsohn and Roy Hart (and even the recently deceased Barry Coghlan) seemed to haunt the place. This visit remains one of the important experiences of my life. I saw some of the best theater I have ever seen and tasted a sweetness of life rarely matched. However this is straying too far from the author and his book, *Dark Voices: The Genesis of Roy Hart Theatre.*

In *Dark Voices*, Noah Pikes has assembled for the first time a narrative which traces not only the stories of Alfred Wolfsohn and Roy Hart, but also a cast of characters as they moved through his life and psyche and the lives of Wolfsohn and Hart. It is a remarkable thing that he has been able to put it all together in a coherent work. If in places it does not hold as tightly as it should, it is probably because Pikes has a romantic tendency to focus on the weak points of the narrative—the fissures of soul—and not build an Apollonic structure worthy of Boswell or assemble disguised memories *à la* Proust. Still I believe this volume and its subsequent one will help make this new "Africa" series unique and will contribute another facet to the legacy of this last century's cultural importance.

Jay Livernois
Zürich, May 1999

EDITOR'S NOTE TO THE NEW EDITION: The editor and publisher would like to thank all those readers who suggested corrections and improvements to the original edition.

Jay Livernois
Eranos, July 2004

Dennis (Noah) Pikes, aged six months, giving voice.

CHAPTER ONE
The Lessons Begin

Oune evening in the winter of 1967 things were terrible. I had smoked a lot of hashish and felt desperate. I consulted the *I Ching*[1] and asked where my life was going. When I had finished throwing the coins, I received Hexagram 29, *The Abyss Beyond the Abyss*. It seemed to be telling me exactly where I was.

At this point I decided to write to Roy Hart, the leader of a group whose members were "working on themselves" by using voice. Hart's own voice was said to cover all the notes of the piano, and supposedly this reflected an extraordinary level of self knowledge. I had visited his group twice in the past with my friend Alan Codd, but being moved in a way I could not understand, I had used the excuse of having the flu to no longer attend. This time I wanted it to work. My letter to Hart ended:

> I have something in me which is God's, but how to express it
> and in what form I cannot see. I am too low. But unless I do
> I may as well give up living and that I cannot do. The ego is
> squirming, trying to keep me from you. I must come to the
> studio as soon as possible. Please, will you accept me?

Two days later I called to see if I could attend the next meeting. A woman with a German accent answered the phone and said firmly, "Roy agrees to your coming, but you must be present at all meetings and on time. Colds are no excuse, and if you want to learn to sing then you will have to stop taking drugs." My game was up. I knew that I had no

[1] Editor's note: This is the classic book of Chinese divination. It became popular in the counter-culture of the 60s with the publication (in 1957) of the Bollingen edition of the Wilhelm/Baynes translation with a foreword by C. G. Jung. It seems that the edition consulted here, though, was the John Blofeld translation.

choice, and I was relieved to be going again to visit this group who met in a soundproofed room in a London suburb. Who were these people? What was this "singing?" Hart described this diverse "family" in 1967:

> This family is a hybrid collection: professional dancers and actors, a trained psychiatrist, successful businessmen, civil servants, schoolteachers, typists, housewives, single, married, married and separate; some with, some without children: homosexuals, heterosexuals; so-called stable and well-adjusted, so-called unstable and neurotic. Six of the thirty present members have a previous history of psychoneurosis; three have been under psycho-analytical treatment prior to joining the family—one is a bad stammerer, who had previously tried various treatments without success. I believe this family's growing understanding and cohesion has saved several of the "neurotics" from hospitalisation and, in one case, from an intended fourth attempt at suicide (where the third attempt was drastic enough). It has likewise saved many of its apparently normal members from smug and irresponsible acceptance of themselves as "normal." Their ages range from 22 to 46. They come from differing deeply religious and from irreligious backgrounds; from the Commonwealth, Europe and the USA. Some have forfeited good homes, some temptingly better chances in their careers, to remain knit to this new family with its purposive way of living.
>
> Most of these people were not naturally gregarious or prone to follow a leader: yet they chose to subject themselves to each other and not (as some at first thought) to me, but, in fact, both they and I are subject to the creative research work we do—to the principle of an eight octave voice. We find that any normal human voice, male or female, usually reckoned to have a range of from two to two and a half octaves, may be extended, by training, to six or more octaves, gaining in expressiveness and emotional content in the process. We have come to study the voice through seemingly chance meetings and for apparently overtly abstruse reasons.[2]

---

[2] "How a Voice Gave me a Conscience" by Roy and Dorothy Hart, a paper for the 7th International Congress of Psychotherapy held at Wiesbaden, August 1967. The theme was the relationship of society to humanity and the role of creative art as preventive medicine.

The group met in a studio located in the London suburb of Golders Green in the home of Hart's wife, Dorothy Hart.[3] This was home not only to Roy and Dorothy but to several other people. There was Jonathan, Dorothy's ten year old son whose father was a Catholic and a former Tanzanian tribal chief who had been centrally involved in negotiating his country's independence. Then there was Derek Rosen, a former chemical engineering student from South Africa who had become a professional dancer in West End musicals and now worked as a civil servant. And there was Marita Günther, one of the earliest members of the group, who had come to Britain from Germany shortly after World War II and who was a distant cousin of Hart's voice teacher, Alfred Wolfsohn. There was Robert Harvey, an Australian dancer who now sang and danced in West End shows such as *Pyjama Game* and *Annie Get Your Gun*. And there was also Kaya Anderson, born in China of a Scottish medical doctor and English mother. She had lived for some time in Rome and was working as a foreign language teacher. These last four were in their thirties or early forties. Dorothy was from a Scottish family who had emigrated to Kenya early in the century, had owned a coffee plantation, and had left only a few years earlier following Kenya's independence. Hart himself came from South Africa and was the son of Jewish parents from Poland. He had studied English and psychology, but his gift and desire was to be an actor, a profession not appreciated by his family. Soon after the Second World War, he had come to London and studied at the Royal Academy of Dramatic Arts (RADA).

Although I was no stranger to outsider groups in Britain, this one was different from my previous experiences, and I was nervous. I came from a family rooted in working class values. My mother bore considerable resentment towards wealthy, privileged, or even well-spoken people and I, too, held some of these values. At Birmingham University I had aligned myself with left-wing, pacifist, and anarchist ideas and groups. I led a group called the University Campaign for Nuclear Disarmament, marched from Aldermaston, and was part of the 1962 sit-down protest led by Bertrand Russell outside the Ministry of Defence. While at university I lived in a rundown area of Birmingham inhabited mainly by immigrants from India, Pakistan, Ireland, the Caribbean, and Africa. I

---

[3] At 41, The Ridgeway.

had been especially close to this last group. By the time I finally dropped out of university at twenty-three, I saw the world from the perspective of a victim and identified with the oppressed of this world. As a result I cultivated a taste for the avant-garde, the absurd, and the obscene.

It was with this attitude that I arrived at Golders Green, and I looked at other members of the group suspiciously. It seemed that several members as well as Hart were Jewish, and although I had identified with Jews as a victimised people, I felt conflicted about their religious practices and stereotypical association with material wealth. Three members of the group were from South Africa whose apartheid policies I detested. I was nervous and on the defensive as I entered the house. Possessed by anxiety, voices in my head said things like; "It smells strange. There are real paintings on the walls. Quite a few foreigners…which are the Jewish ones? Some strange accents. Even a bit upper class. And that one is definitely homosexual. Oh! A double breasted blazer!" My anxiety was eased by Alan's presence and a few people my own age. In a quiet way a couple of people asked my name and told me theirs.

Precisely at quarter-to-seven, the door of the studio opened from the inside. The group of about twenty-five silently entered, one by one. I stayed close to Alan and was amazed to notice a second, padded door. I later learned that the room itself was an inner shell within the original room, and such innovations in a suburban setting intrigued me. The room had a sofa and some chairs around the walls. There were more paintings and large floral curtains covering French windows opposite the entrance. To the right of them stood an upright piano piled high with stacks of music.

At the piano was a big-bodied, suntanned man in his forties. He had a broad face and brown hair combed back. He wore tan cavalry twill trousers (which I disliked for their military and upper-class connotations) and well polished brown shoes. He was seated in a high-backed swivel chair. His presence dominated the room and it both threatened and comforted me. There was something in his eyes that gave me the feeling that I was being seen through. Yet this was not the drugged-out, paranoid feeling I had been getting so often recently. There was compassion in Hart's eyes, too.

The atmosphere in the room was concentrated and focused, and Hart maintained control despite the fact that he never left his swivel chair during the entirety of the session. Most of that first visit was spent discussing the dreams of a few of the group members. After a while Hart asked me a question. "Dennis," he said in his deep resonant voice, "do you masturbate?" Shocked and embarrassed I replied, "Well, yes, occasionally, but I'm trying to cut it out." He retorted, "I suggest rather that you should try to enjoy it more often." Then he added, "Personally, however, I prefer the real thing."

At around 10 P.M. Hart gently played a chord on the piano and held the last note. It was a sign for each person to sing the word "A-dee-o" slowly, lingering on each syllable. It was to be done all on that one note and to be done so directly to another person. During the in-breath, everyone turned to find a new partner as Hart played another chord and the singing good-bye was repeated. Much to my embarrassment I was included. Although it was a simple and human parting, I wanted to flee.

This embarrassment was part of my general resistance to the group and became a frequent feeling over the next few meetings. Internally, I distanced myself from the other members of the group: "Are these what enlightened people are like? No one seems very hip. Quite a lot of odd balls here. And some of them have definitely got money, even unearned income, I'm sure. Capitalists." Yet another part of me was appreciating the feeling of family, the careful quality of communication, and the physical contact. I felt a warmth from Dorothy Hart and liked her spontaneous way with Roy, every so often countering an assertion or helping someone who might have been made to feel vulnerable. There was a certain sense of teamwork between the members of the group, although Hart's leadership was never in doubt. I liked their ideas about art and self-expression which Roy and Dorothy described as attainable even by those without "artistic gifts."

> One of the most pressing problems of our day is to redefine the whole meaning of Art and artistic gifts. Has the creative impulse only to be considered the possession of a hierarchy of gifted people, musicians, painters and so on? Or must we rediscover the intrinsic common factor behind the creative impulse? Many so-called untalented people, factory hands, office workers or manual labourers, have been demoralised out of all sense of their own creative potential; and the diffidence thus imposed on them results in serious

misuse of their leisure hours. I could write another twenty-minute paper on the significance of the pop group rage. In primitive society, the creative, artistic urge was shared in by all and given dignity in religious rituals. And crafts too had a religious significance, down to the poorest domestic utensil. It is significant that a great number of people in our society want to be actors or painters, amateurs if not professional. They desperately desire their efforts to be taken seriously, and pathetically they glut the market. When we learn to value the clumsiest creativity of our human acquaintances, and honour their most tentative gropings, they become our friends.

We believe that the greatest contributing force to mental breakdown is the lack of outlet for truthful self-expression, tolerance of this expression by others and courage to persevere in it for oneself. The medium we have chosen can safely contain the variety of man's emotions without crushing him....

We present only one way of enabling ordinary people to explore their own creativity, (keeping a careful balance between physical and mental exertion) that we have experienced as wholly beneficial—the experience of finding our multiple voices in an ever-increasing range with concomitant side effects in our daily living.

"And this secret spoke Life Herself to me, 'Behold' said she, 'I am that which must ever surpass itself'...." F. Nietzsche.[4]

Several sessions later the reserve I had maintained broke down when Hart asked a man and a woman to enact a rape scene. I am now convinced it was enacted for me, although that was not said. I witnessed real and extremely physical action and voices. The woman was struggling hard as the man forced her to the ground. She screamed, "Let me go!" But he pinned her hands down on the floor, making loud and aggressive sounds. This scene was utterly convincing and yet totally acted. No clothes were removed or even opened. While no actual sexual contact happened, this short scene opened the floodgates of my heart. I broke down and wept as I had not since childhood. The next day Marita phoned me. "Roy sends you this message," she said. "What happened last night was very important. One day your voice will be a great asset to the group. You should begin singing lessons with Lizzie."

[4] *Op. cit.* "How Voice Gave Me a Conscience," Roy and Dorothy Hart, 1967.

Chapter Two

Early Years

I was born in wartime London to a frightened young mother under the glaring lamps and eyes of a dozen pediatric students. My first scream seems to have announced my calling in life. Or maybe my bent for using my voice came from my father who was from a long line of hot-tempered, Welsh-border wheelwrights and coffin makers. Or maybe it came from the fact that at the time of my birth, nutrition specialists had deemed mother's milk unsuitable, and so I was separated from my mother for twenty-four hours during which time I made full use of my vocal expression. The screaming worked, and I was breast fed for a time, yet it was only allowed to be once every four hours. I learned these things a few years prior to my mother's suicide at sixty-nine following her many years of struggle with schizophrenia and the death of her second husband. She had written me and told me of my birth, her own trauma, and my frequent crying. She apologised if this had been a cause for difficulties later in my life.

My parents, Alice and Cecil, were both Londoners. Alice was one of five children born to working class parents. Her mother, May Pegg, worked as a domestic helper, and I recall her being generous and friendly, often sending three or six pence for me in her occasional letters to the family. Alice's father, John, was a factory worker with a smoker's voice and cockney accent. The few times I met him were visits on holidays or weekends to their terraced house in Coventry. He would return from the pub in a cloud of beer and smoke fumes, put on his slippers, and disappear behind a newspaper in front of the coal fire. Before long he would be snoring.

My mother had been a bright child and a strong swimmer. It was a source of pride for me to see the silver cup and her thirteen medals for wins during her school days displayed on the piano. It must have been her talent as a swimmer that lay behind her passion to live near the sea as soon as she could escape London. She also loved walking, and I have fond memories of strolls among the cowslips and daffodils, woods and fields, or along the beach or cliff tops of Devon. She taught me that there was a world to discover beyond school and home.

My father, though christened Cecil, was known by everyone as Cyril because he felt the connotations of "Cecil" were too "sissy." Having been born out of wedlock, he was brought up by an aunt who was married. These circumstances must have been troubling for him as it was only when I was in my thirties that I was told a distant aunt was his real mother. As a child I had often missed the second grandmother that my peers all seemed to have, and her absence contributed to the feeling that somehow our family differed from the others in our small town. It seems that Cecil's father was a former professional footballer who ran a sports shop in Derby. He had once or twice taken his son out for the day, but there was never any substance to their relationship. I never missed my second grandfather though.

My father worked as a toolmaker, and his return home in the evening was accompanied by the smell of oil and metal shavings. He later told me that he had wanted to be a carpenter, but things being what they were, he had been obliged to accept an apprenticeship as a tool and die maker. But he combined the elements of wood and metal and learned to play the guitar as a teenager, swinging in 1940s dance band style. Occasionally, when he overcame his embarrassment, he sang with a voice rather trapped in his throat. Usually he just whistled the melody as he played.

When I was about seven, some fellow musicians came to our sitting room one day to run through some numbers. I was fascinated by the incisive sticks, caressing brushes, and the magic movements of the drummer's hi-hat and bass drum pedal. The zest of the piano player who joined in was different to my mother's playing and the mechanical piano lessons I had just begun. I saw for the first time a male energy in music, and a seed of longing for musical expression began to grow within me.

Apart from his rare moments of violent temper and less rare sarcasm towards my mother, my father was a gentle man and fun to be with. He cultivated a moral and responsible attitude, never drank to excess, and was active in the Buffaloes, a workingman's version of the Freemasons. He was faithful to my mother as far as I know, although she had an affair when she was in her forties. His free time was spent either on his passion for a 1930 Austin 7 with a radiator that would boil over when we drove up the long Devon hills or his duty imposed by Alice to grow vegetables on an allotment outside the town. I would sometimes help with weeding and feed the bonfire, which often frustrated me with its reluctance to flame. Once my father said, "Dennis, you must learn that where there's smoke, there's fire," but I longed for some flames. To this day when I catch that sweet smell of garden fire smoke—so different from burning plastic, cardboard, or rubber—I regress for a moment into my childhood.

The First of Many Moves

We were evacuated from London just after I was born in 1941. The family was sent first to Wales, where I was given the name "Dennis," and then to Devon, where my father worked in an aircraft factory at Honiton, a farming town in peacetime known for its traditional lace-making and eighteenth-century homes. Three years later we moved to Seaton, a small fishing town with a shingled beach nestled in a cliff-held bay that came alive with cawing sea gulls flying overhead. One day not long after we arrived, I felt a warm splatter when a sea gull shat on my head. I later learned that this common occurrence was considered good luck. Bad luck followed though as I was bullied by a boy in hob-nailed boots twice my age in my first year at school.

I certainly shocked my mother on occasion, often with the help of fire. I was fascinated by matches, and I once tried to set fire to a lamp shade. And one Friday evening a few years later, as we sat at the kitchen table, my father handed my mother a little brown envelope containing a £5 note, which was half my father's hard-earned wages. I was intrigued by the large sheet of white paper with elegant black writing, so he handed it to me for a moment. I quickly opened the cover of the nearby coke burner and put it inside.

Luckily, the stove had just been stoked, so there was a layer of unburned fuel on the top, and the note was rescued from the flames.

Upon reflection, I see in this impulse the first seeds of my later rejection of money, a rejection which as a student I identified with politically and philosophically, although I started earning money at the age of ten. At that time I was paid two shillings every Saturday for washing the corridor and entrance our flat shared with a shoe shop. The job seemed like play as I emptied the full bucket of dirty water into the gently sloping street gutter. I enjoyed watching the water momentarily swell like the beginning of a flood. It seemed to my young eyes to require just a few more buckets to drown the whole world.

But childhood was not all work. With my mother's help I learned to swim quite early, and to reward my accomplishment, she gave me a copy of *Alice in Wonderland*. At the age of seven I read "Fitcher's Bird" from *Grimm's Fairy Tales*, a tale of young maidens being dismembered and blood collected in the sink of a small room, although the maidens are well re-membered at the end, and Fitcher is punished for his violent crime. A thrill went through me when I discovered the power of the written word; something sexual, some-thing secretive, and something that awakened dark images in my mind.

In 1945 my sister, Margaret, was born. A few years later we moved away from Seaton, where I had experienced bullying at school, to Milford-on-Sea, in Hampshire, where after school I was often chased by local boys looking for a fist fight. Although I escaped and never fought back, the chicken pox and a fall from a bicycle came as a relief since they gave me a few weeks off from school.

Enter Stage Right

A year later we moved yet again from the wooden house with paraffin lamps to a small bungalow owned by a factory in Lymington where my father worked. The house was in nearby Pennington, and my school changed for the better. It was here that I was first introduced to theatre. Mrs. Shelly, the Headmistress, liked me, and I became her "favourite" and Head Boy of the school. She gave me the lead in *The Pied Piper of Hamlin*, for which a resplendent

Margaret Pikes as a winged fairy and Dennis Pikes as "The Pied Piper," 1951.

costume was made and which we performed for parents and friends. I enjoyed dancing at the weekly country dancing classes held at the Women's Institute Hall. It was mostly a happy time.

Later, daily work and theatre began to merge. At the age of fifteen I delivered meat on Saturdays for a local butcher, a job that was put to creative use in a sketch for the pre-Christmas school show, a yearly event designed to display the emerging and varied talents of the pupils. In it I emerged through the trap door in the floor of the green-lit stage, in front of some five hundred fellow students and teachers, brandishing two huge bones as part of some kind of comic evocation of the Underworld. Perhaps it was this supporting role that later landed me the role of the servant to Nikolai Gogol's "Government Inspector." The boy who played the Inspector, Jonathan Raban, lived in the same village as me and is now a well-known author who wrote of those times in his book, *Coasting*. This was the summit of my official student theatre appearances.

Portrait of a Worker as a Young Man

I began attending local grammar school in Brockenhurst, a small town in the New Forest, at age twelve. My mother wanted me to start earning money delivering newspapers before school but was told this was illegal for children under fourteen. However I soon made up for lost time by biking from our new home in Elerton three miles to Lymington in all weathers, working, then taking the train to school. I also delivered on weekends and added the butcher's job too. During holidays I often took on miserable jobs. One that was particularly unpleasant was for a company called Golden Produce which mass-produced chickens, a new idea at the time in Britain. At first I worked in a battery house, feeding the birds and shovelling out their shit. In a way I was proud to be doing a man's work. But one day, when the hundreds of birds had grown up, I had to help load them into wooden crates and accompany the truck to the packing station. After unloading I was put to work on the conveyor belt, from which two small metal clefts were hanging at one foot intervals. My job was to grab a chicken by its legs from the crate and place them in the two clefts, heads hanging down. A moment later they arrived at a u-turn where an elderly lady slit their throats and held up their heads to allow the first rush of blood to pour into a bucket. After two days of this I had to leave.

My mother believed it important that children learn the value of work at an early age. Despite this, my parents paid for me to go on school trips to Sweden and Spain and to make a three week exchange to France. I was well clothed, and I had a bicycle. I even bought a record every so often. At sixteen my father bought me a clarinet, although my teacher disappeared after two lessons.

Boys and Girls: The Games They Play

A sexual awakening was late in coming. I was forbidden to go to Boy Scout camp because my mother feared homosexuality was rampant there. I seemed to be behind other boys in physical development, and I recoiled from group masturbation on the school train, where other boys of my age competed to see whose ejaculation travelled the furthest. None of my sex education came from my parents. It came from *The Complete Family Self Educator*, where I saw diagrams of human sex organs which provoked my first glimmers of sexual excitement. I mostly learned about sex from other boys while peering into the girls' showers after sports and from groping girls on the train.

At fifteen I had my first sexual experience with a lively girl named Wendy. After a few months of physical exploration, she told me that it was vital that we really do "it." However after several attempts on a blanket in the woods with condoms embarrassingly purchased from the men's hairdresser, her wish remained unfulfilled. She soon left me to marry the son of a local headmaster, and within a year she became pregnant. I was devastated. The experience left me cynical and unable to approach women for many years.

Wendy and Dennis at the beach in Barton-on-Sea

I was thirteen when Rock 'n Roll first hit England; Bill Haley, Little Richard, Fats Domino, Elvis Presley. The music felt like a life-line from over the ocean, and I collected more than fifty such names, written on the inside of my desk lid at school, to be shared with a few other rockers. I heard them on *Rockin' to Dreamland*, under the bed covers on an early pirate radio station from Luxembourg. Although my audible models were mostly the voices and music of black men, my visible ones were the swashbuckling, white heroes like Errol Flynn and John Wayne. I was an avid fan and (mediocre) practitioner of both football and cricket, whose pantheon of stars also provided unattainable images of manhood, and I harbored secret fantasies that I was actually a great talent awaiting someone with perception adequate enough to discover it.

While I was learning about alcohol and cigarettes, I saw my first "dirty" pictures on a school trip to Sweden. Black and white breasts, bums and pubic hair—this latter banned by the government at home— all dangling like tantalising fruits from the upper branches of Stockholm's street kiosks. It was on this trip that I fell in with "Snuggy" Moores and Jim Insole, two fellow Brockenhurst pupils. We started a kind of a linguistic and theatrical research project in which we would greet passersby in a friendly manner, smiling and using a warm tone of voice, while uttering as obscene a string of verbal garbage as we could muster. Thus, "Good morning you shit faced bum licking wanked out pisspot of a cesspit" said with choirboy innocence and a Hampshire accent, usually evoked a warm and friendly reply in Swedish. Soon I joined these boys in singing folk songs like "The Midnight Special," "The Red Flag," or "Careless Love" to the accompaniment of Snug's banjo and several glasses of "scrumpy," a rough West Country cider. This way we enlivened many a dull evening in local pubs, and later, nearby streets.

Snuggy and Jim became part of my emerging all-male "alterna-tive" peer group that included two other friends, John McWilliam and Jeremy Hooker. John had an original mind, hated Brockenhurst Grammar School, and left at sixteen to "work on the buildings." Although he had a spell in a mental hospital, he was extremely perceptive about people's motives and their behavior and could be bitingly sarcastic about the hypocrisy he observed. In this respect I admired him greatly, even though I sometimes became the butt of his observations. He was exciting to be around because I never knew what to expect from him. For instance, one day he showed me a painting he had recently completed using powder paint mixed with his own semen. He claimed to be bisexual, and according to his stories at least, seemed to have no difficulty with women, claiming to have seduced more than one young married lady who was bored with her husband. Jerry also had success with the ladies, partly because of his angular good looks. However, he went through considerable anguish on their account, a process that he often expressed by writing poetry.[1] John also wrote poetry, and both he and Jerry fed me the literature of Henry Miller and Kenneth Patchen, Bertrand Russell and Karl Marx, Kerouac and Beat poetry, and the music of Sidney Bechet and Be-bop.

My political rebellion began when it was announced that my state-funded school, which had pretensions towards a private school style, would be creating a military cadet force to prepare pupils for eventual entry into the services as officers. In what must have been part of my then unconscious quest for initiation into manhood, I joined the soldier cadet force. Every Friday we came to school in our full military dress to attend drill sessions and evening classes. Meanwhile Jerry Hooker introduced me to socialism and antinuclear ideas. He gave me a newly created Campaign for Nuclear Disarmament (CND) badge, and I began to wear this on my school blazer. While at first there seemed to be no reason not to put it on my soldier's outfit on Fridays, these two pieces of gear, as well as my own views, were judged to be incompatible. I chose to drop out of the cadets.

My grades earned me a place at Birmingham University in central England to study civil engineering. In my first week, while waiting in the bursar's office to receive an advance on my grant, Spencer Davis,[2] a tall Welsh student there for the same purpose, began to play a Blues guitar. I had never heard a twelve string before, and when he burst into "San Francisco Bay" I was mesmerised. This was just what I imagined university would be like. But I soon felt uncomfortable in the class-

---

[1] Jeremy Hooker is now the author of seven books and a professor of English literature.

[2] Spencer Davis went on to lead one of Britain's popular R&B groups along with local (Birmingham) singer Steve Winwood.

room. I was amongst fifty "rugger buggers" whose main interests outside of studies were beer, rugby, and women. I felt comfortable among left-wing radicals, CND protesters, and jazz lovers. They were studying social science, philosophy, or literature. These were subjects I had barely heard about. State education was so generous at that time that I was permitted to change course and return the following year to begin studying "Moral and Political Philosophy."

I became chairman of the University CND movement and attended many meetings of left-wing groups. I eventually found Anarchism the most appealing, where the idea of external government is rejected in favour of education adequate enough to enable individuals to make their own decisions. While I learned about the soul in Plato's *Republic* and of other notions basic to the "humanities," something seemed to be missing in my own humanity. Around this time I came across a copy of a book by C. G. Jung called *Modern Man in Search of a Soul*. I did not understand much at the time, but the title stayed with me over the years and seemed to speak to me.

I was loosely part of a circle of jazz loving lefties that included Dick Hewitson, a local botany student who had a beard, a noncompetitive attitude, and an eccentric sense of humor. He was just the

Front (left to right): Heather Goldsborough, Anne Petter, Dick Hewitson.
Back: unknown, Dave Chaney, Andy Miller, Charles Guest.

kind of person I dreamed of meeting at university. The circle also included Heather, a girl from Manchester who was studying law. Heather and I eyed each other for a few weeks across the coffee tables, and we soon moved on to cuddling in the evening at Dick's house.

Breakfast in Bed

Inspired by Henry Miller's *Colossus of Marroussi,* Heather and I convinced each other to drop out of university and hitchhike to Greece to "find ourselves." After three days and two short nights of sleeping rough, we were left late one night by a motorist on a country lane in the heel of Italy, too far from Brindisi to hope to get another lift. We walked down the lane a few hundred yards, laid out our sleeping bags in a field under an olive tree, and fell asleep. As we awoke there was bright sunlight and the amused looks of a stream of local residents walking or biking along the lane. Heather then spotted someone approaching us and carrying something in front of him. We were uneasy about his intentions as he got closer until we saw the object he was carrying. It was a breakfast tray, complete with bread, butter, boiled eggs, jam, coffee, cups, and saucers. He put it at our feet, greeted us warmly, then walked back. It was a magical moment and we were amazed.

We spent the next night in a hotel near Brindisi, and with the few lira we still had, we ate in the hotel restaurant. I ordered a wine called, "Lacryma dei Cristi," that had effects Henry Miller once admired. We drank the whole bottle and retired to the bedroom. At last, went my fantasy, we are going to fuck. It began promisingly. This was the first time we had lain naked together and gone beyond the flirtatious suggestion of a sexual encounter. As it approached the "real" thing, and I was about to enter her, Heather resisted and pushed me away, telling me "no." I was shattered. It seems that we both could not talk about sex, and the lack of a condom probably exacerbated the problem. Over the next few days, while I fell into a sulk, Heather enjoyed herself playing cards and flirting with a group of local men.

In our penniless state we garnered the support of a Greek diplomat we met as he was returning to Athens. He lent us the boat fare to cross to Igouminitsa and gave us his address to come and stay once we arrived in Athens. This we did by hitchhiked truck, much of the journey done under cool moonlight with the headlights off. We stayed for a week at a flat the diplomat shared with his mother, until one day he took us to a place he had rented for us on Lykavitos Street. It was unbelievably generous and crazy, just as Henry Miller had promised. He arranged work for us in a nearby language school, and soon we were able to pay our own rent. A month or so later several university friends came out to join us for the summer, sleeping on the floor of our flat.

By this time, of course, the romance between Heather and me was not going well, and she began to spend time with a young man working in a nearby bank. But that ended after he took us to an island for a weekend. He rented donkeys, and we rode under the moonlight at night, and slept, swam, and drank wine on the beach during the day. When we returned to Athens, he was arrested for theft from his bank. It did not matter, however. At the end of summer, I returned to England alone.

Although I left Heather behind, the adventures continued. I got a lift outside of Rome from a young man who was joyriding in his father's car. After a few miles he began swerving across the road, driving fast, and trying to scare me. Suddenly, with no more than a quick bump, we were upside down and skidding to a halt on the roof of the car. Stunned and upside down, I managed to open the door and fall out onto the road. The young driver went crazy and started screaming that I was responsible for ruining his father's car. I was to *va via* as fast as possible. Eventually getting my bag from the dented boot, I walked off down the road leaving him swearing.

Suffering from what I now believe was a concussion, I felt unwell and unable to continue travelling that evening. I stayed two nights in a *Zimmer* in Austria. Later travelling through Switzerland, a forty year-old woman in a Mercedes picked me up, drove to a hotel, and invited me in. I am not sure now if I was still unwell, found her unattractive, or was just plain frightened, but I pretended not to understand what she wanted from me, much to her annoyance.

I eventually made it to Birmingham and became a bus conductor. So much for "finding myself."

Birmingham

Birmingham remained my home for about a year while I hung out with a group of jazz loving students and musicians. One of them was Evan Parker, a sax-playing botany student who led a quartet playing John Coltrane's avant-garde jazz. Jazz became a lifeline for me. Its energy, roots, philosophy, and people felt like an international family. Part of that family was Pete Burden who played alto sax like Charlie Parker with a touch of Jackie MacLean. It was he who "turned me on" to "pot," and the "hipster's" language. He had spent time in Toronto with a black musician and knew the "cool" way to think and talk. I would often meet up with him in London and once arranged a gig for him with Evan in Birmingham.

Birmingham was also the home of Africans, mostly from Nigeria, who had settled there after the war, and I befriended several of them. One man in particular, Gabby Ojo, worked the early shift in the Birmingham City Corporation Refuse Disposal factory. I took some Charlie Parker records to his house one day, and seeing his enjoyment of the music, I went on frequent visits. Nights of intoxication in the pubs of Balsall Heath made me wish I were African, and Gabby became a kind of surrogate father initiating me into male society; a thing that my real father could not provide.

Another friend was Olu, a big man who was married to a small Irish woman named Cathy. They had two young children, and I moved into a room in the house where they lived, on Pershore Road. One night over dinner, Olu and Cathy told me that Reecie, a pretty, sixteen year-old, dark skinned girl of Caribbean immigrant parents wanted to meet me. I had only glimpsed her once on the stairs and was startled to find her waiting for me in my small room when I came home the next evening. When I entered she was silently leaning against the wall, her body trembling. I quickly realized that she wanted to explore her blossoming sexuality, with me as her teacher. This seemed to work, though I had precious little to teach. After a couple of weeks of mutual exploration, Reecie and I went the "whole way," and I experienced my first orgasm with a woman. But having worn no condom, I grew scared she would become pregnant and ran away the next day to my parents' house, still a mummy's boy at heart. I did return to her, shamefaced, a few weeks later, only to discover that she had been moved to a convent. When I finally found her and apologised, she told me it was over.

To Africa

Gabby set me up with a job as a British Railways truck driver, a job I kept for about six months until my *wanderlust* returned. Africa was calling, and counting on my experience as a hitchhiker, I planned a trip to Gabby's homeland. Money seemed to be no object as I had heard that there were regular groups of trucks and cars crossing the Sahara, from Tangier to Nigeria. Taking a few simple things and little money, I left Birmingham for another adventure.

The first stop was Paris, where I stayed for ten days in George Whitman's English language book shop, "Shakespeare and Company," where it was considered an honor to sleep in the visiting writer's quarters above the store. George Whitman is a generous and cryptic man, and I enjoyed helping him out in the book shop for a few hours a day. However, since the caravans to West Africa left only once a month, I spent much of my savings buying hashish and trying to find another way to the Dark Continent.

Despite my limited French, I tracked down a German cargo ship heading to ports in the former French colonies. The ship's director offered me a much reduced student price, for which I would have a cabin to myself and three excellent German meals at the captain's table. Disappointed that the ship was not calling at Lagos, Nigeria, I planned to hitch to Lagos from the nearest port-of-call, Lomé, Togo. I joined the boat at Rouen, and we sailed immediately for Tenerife, the largest of the Canary Islands.

Sailing onward after Tenerife, I visited the market in Dakar, and after a four-day wait in the harbor of Conakry, the capital of Guinea, I was able to go for a swim in a hot and unrefreshing sea. On the trip I had occasional conversations with an elderly German pastor who was on his way to visit Albert Schweizer's hospital in Cameroon. These conversations were not easy. He could speak a little French and I spoke no German. In addition, he was deaf, and in order to talk, he had to first turn on a hearing aid with a microphone mounted on his chest. I had to speak close to the microphone on his chest so that he could hear me, making visual contact with his face nearly impossible. These exchanges were among the few I experienced in what was a boring voyage.

By the time we arrived in Lomé, I had insufficient funds to pay for my journey. How I extricated myself from that situation I do not remember. What I do recall well, however, is how I landed and the journey to Lagos. At that time in 1964, Togo had no port, so the ship put down anchor about two hundred yards off shore. There was a consignment of huge sacks of flour which were off-loaded a few at a time in wide, meshed rope netting into circular shaped barges. I and my meagre belongings were lowered atop one such load and ferried to the shore.

Once ashore, I prepared to hitchhike along the three hundred miles of coastline that lay between Lomé and Lagos. A German engineer working on the construction of a port financed by his government told me that one could not do that here. He said there were dangers I was not aware of, and offering to help me get there another way, he and his family welcomed me into their home. Two days later he and I set out for Cotonou along the mostly dirt track that led across the border to the capital of Dahomey, now Benin. Once there I waited, sitting in a large old taxi which, when full, would make the seventy mile drive through the bush to Lagos. Many hours later the taxi was jam packed and its roof laden with our belongings. The taxi wound its way through several villages to drop off passengers and take on new ones. That evening I arrived at the house of Gabby's boyhood friend, Samuel White. Sam had suffered from polio as a boy, and one of his legs was withered, although he was not lacking in vigour. By no means a wealthy man, he welcomed me into his modest home. I stayed with him for close to three months.

Since I had no money, I found a school ready to employ me as a teacher. All that was needed for employment was a certain paper. But, contrary to what I had been told by Nigerian officials in London, I learned that this paper could not be obtained in Nigeria, only prior to departure in London. So instead of working I spent the time "hanging out," smoking marijuana, drinking beer, and listening to "high life" music while my sister Margaret made a collection of money

Samuel White plays games with Dennis Pikes in Lagos 1964.

amongst friends in Birmingham. She sent me the money, and I returned to London with a ticket furnished by the British Foreign Office for which my passport was confiscated, only to be returned when I had repaid the fare. I hoped to make a dent in this debt by selling half a pound of powerful Nigerian "grass" I had hidden under my clothing. However, only a small part of it was sold. A good portion went to Gabby and his friends, and the rest went up in smoke with my other pals. The end result of the trip was the painful realisation that I was not an African, and a big part of my "wannabe" fantasy was dissolved.

Petty Crime as Social Anarchy

From 1964 on I seemed to flail around, rejecting any kind of career, taking only bum jobs at a beer factory and as a shop assistant or delivery man. I hated to be under the thumbs of what I saw as petty, working-class dictators. I slid further beyond social and familial boundaries by drifting into petty fraud and gambling. Wallowing in the back waters of the 1960's student unrest and fed by the explosion in popular culture and music, I made contacts with other slippery souls. One of the other "fish" I met there was a literature student, Alan Codd, who was writing a thesis on Samuel Becket. (We were to eventually pair up and share a flat together. The flat bell was labelled "Pikes & Codd." I met Alan through Evan Parker, and the three of us worked together one summer in the catering department of Eagle Airways while Graeme, another friend of Evan's, worked in baggage handling. When we met up at home, Graeme would often show us cameras, razors, and clothing which he had lifted from people's luggage. He was later Bryan Ferry's first bass player in Roxy Music.

Soon after that, in Birmingham, I met Jim Davis who introduced me to the arts of writing stolen cheques. Under his tutelage, I learned about the profits to be had from "hot" goods. We would make expeditions with the cheques to a town, buy clothes that had been ordered by others we knew, or musical instruments and other sale-able items, which we then sold in local secondhand shops to give us cash. This work was far more challenging, exciting, and rewarding than the dead-end jobs I would have been working in, and I developed a certain proficiency at it.

I justified the thievery by convincing myself it was anarchism in practice. If I ever considered the distress such theft must have caused to the cheque owners or shops, I dismissed it with thoughts about the "rottenness of the whole capitalist system" and told myself that "anyway such people can well afford it." From there, I learned to defraud American Express, via its Traveller's Cheques, which seemed at the time to be a more anarchistic and ethical way to do those things. On the second outing, though, they kept me waiting for some hours in an Antwerp office, and when I eventually got paid, I hurtled to the airport, on the way deciding fraud was too risky.

The Mysterious Organisation

Alan was studying at Newcastle University at this time, as was Vivienne Young, the best friend of Margaret, my sister. Her mother, Mary, lived at Milford-on-Sea and was one of the few friends of my mother's. The relationship that grew between Vivienne and Alan is part of what Roy Hart would later refer to as "the mysterious organisation of minute matter." There were others at Newcastle who would later know Hart, including Richard Armstrong, who was then studying painting alongside Vivienne.

One day in 1965 Jim Davis and I decided to visit Newcastle. In the day we would "go shopping" with a full-order book from the circle of students there, and in the evening enjoy the night life of the town. The town seemed full of artistic people. At a book reading I met Robert Creeley, who dutifully signed my copy of his novel, *The Island*. Another evening was spent in a club where a then-unknown local R&B group called "The Animals" was playing. Margaret (who was studying at Hull University) and Vivienne were there, and danced with the band's singer, Eric Burdon, and we drank pints of Newcastle Brown Ale.

Although this was the first time I was part of a group of artistic people, I felt blocked. I felt like I was living vicariously through other people; a voyeur, a sham, a petty criminal, a wanking wannabe. Sex to me was elusive. While Evan gave me copies of early *Playboy* magazines (which he got via his air-hostess sister on her return flights from the United States), I felt alienated from women. Apart from Reecie, photos were the closest I got to a female body for years. I was twenty-three, and it seemed to me that the gods conspired to make sure that I would be frustrated.

Meeting the Monsters

When I first read of hallucinogens, I knew right away that they were what I needed to make my break-out, or break-in—or as it evolved, breakdown. I read about Timothy Leary and his colleagues at Harvard University who had experimented with LSD. A new translation of the *Tibetan Book of the Dead* had just been published, and they recommended that one study it using LSD. I bought a copy, and through friends in London, I met a man named Robert who not only dealt in good quality hashish from Lebanon but said he would shortly be in possession of a quantity of potent LSD.

He was and it was. A demon was calling, and I took off into the night where the light was dazzling like a nuclear fission. I was gone for eight hours, no body there, dining with the gods at the centre of the Void. For some months after discovering LSD, I felt great, regenerated, full of insights, and peaceful feelings. I even studied for and passed the first year Moral and Political Philosophy exams which enabled me to re-enter the course.

But there was more in store for me. I was about to meet with a loss of innocence. And I would soon learn that there is no initiation without a prolonged visit to the underworld, without facing the monsters within me.

My friends and I held LSD and pot parties at a house we lived in on Rotton Park Road, Birmingham. Alan Codd, who became a frequent visitor, had obtained a high level degree and was now engaged on a master's thesis at nearby Warwick University. At the same time his visits became less frequent, Alan's friendship became more important to me as the dross of my situation thickened. While he had managed to find a way through academia, I had dropped out again. I could no longer focus enough to put thoughts on paper and into sentences, let alone write an essay. I sought help from the University Medical Service, but I found no relief. My mind longed for a discipline. I tried transcendental meditation, but I found it only took me further from my body and mind and it seemed to dissolve what little solid ground I had. I devoured books on all kinds of esoteric paths and was drawn to Sufism, but I could find no teacher in Europe at that time. I read all of the books on and by Gurdjieff, but the atmosphere emanating from the Gurdjieff group in London did not attract me. These readings remained as vague ideas, loosely floating on pink strawberry fields. I had no idea how to make them real. Instead of providing me with a depth of experience, LSD trips revealed an absence in me. There was no soul and no mantra meditations produced it. I later discovered that soul is not given, it has to be made.

A Man Called Roy Hart

I was becoming desperate, and one day about six months after I discovered LSD, I visited Alan in his flat in Leamington Spa. It was clear that something in him had changed. He was more focused in an adult sort of way, and he kept me at a distance. He did not want to smoke or drink. He told me he had met a man called Roy Hart who worked with voice and used it as a tool for psychological growth; for work on oneself. I had vaguely heard of this man, and work on oneself was something the Greco-Armenian mystic, Gurdjieff, advocated. Alan told me the work was important for him and for Vivienne, who now had a friendship with Richard Armstrong. It seemed that they were all going to Roy Hart's studio in London.

Alan played me a tape of Hart demonstrating his voice, interpreting a passage from T. S. Eliot's poem, "The Rock." I was shocked
and puzzled by what I heard. Hart made sounds unlike voices I had
ever heard, sounds that evoked elements, animals, emotions, and
mystery. Although I could not have articulated this at the time, the
impression was of "otherness." There was a strength and presence, a
conscious intention in the articulation and modulations of intonation,
and above all the message that this man knew what he was doing.
What he said in his extraordinary way was moving:

> ...men, in their various ways, they struggled in torment
> towards GOD.
> ...man is a vain thing and man without GOD is a seed
> upon the wind, driven this way and that, and finding no
> place of lodgement and germination.
> Through the Passion and Sacrifice saved in spite of
> their negative being.
> But it seems that something has happened that has
> never happened before: though we know not just when or
> why or how or where. Men have left GOD...

Although the tape Alan played for me shook me, I slipped further
into emotional despair, becoming dependent on my friends and
growing paranoid. I had been living in a room in Pete Burdon's flat,
in a house full of some of London's leading jazz musicians near
London's Earl's Court. I was fixated on Pete, as if he were my
father, therapist, and guru. Eventually John Mumford, a trombonist,
told me firmly that I should leave that house and let Pete get on with
his life. It was at this time that I wrote the letter to Roy Hart.

Singing for My Life

My first singing lesson was in the studio at Golders Green with
Elisabeth Meyer (Lizzie). It had been years since I had sung. Even
the bawdy pub songs, folk favourites, and daily hymns at school assem-
bly were a distant memory. Yet as I thought about it, there were a few
that echoed in my ear like *Immortal, Invisible, God Only Wise*. Lizzie, who
had worked with Hart for five years, was sitting at the piano as I
entered the studio. She was a tall, attractive blonde about thirty years

Between rehearsal and a river, standing: Nadine Silber, Elizabeth Mayer; sitting (left to right): Kevin Crawford, Heide Hildebrand, Derek Rosen, Louis Frenkel.

old. Born in Berlin, nursed in Lausanne, and raised in Haiti, she held a degree in history from Radcliff College (Harvard's sister school). Her father was an American diplomat.

Lizzie's attitude was a little stern and detached, yet not lacking in warmth. (I later discovered that I was one of her first pupils and represented something of a challenge.) The sounds she wanted from me were not what I had heard on Alan's tape. What she wanted seemed to me more like shouting and calling out. But the lesson made memories flash into my mind. I recalled the enjoyment I had felt in singing loudly at football matches, and later on the CND marches where we shouted chants like, "U.S. Bases! Out! Out! Out!"

But there was work to do. Lizzie would give me a note on the piano, and I had to repeat the same sound on different notes as she moved up the scale and down again. She would demand more volume until, high up the scale, the sound would become broken, the note sometimes lost, my voice jumping out of control. But as long as I concentrated and tried for the note, it was accepted. What she wanted most from me was that I put bodily energy into my voice.

Over the months as I delivered laundry to earn my living, Lizzie pushed, pulled, and shook me during our weekly lessons for my voice to, "Come out, come out!" She demanded that I fill the room with my voice—to cross the walls erected by shyness, laziness, and bitchiness—and I sometimes wanted none of it. She forced me to connect my voice to my rejected body and suppressed anger. It was exhilarating, irritating, exhausting, and I usually left sweating.

A calmness that came at the end of each lesson did not always last long, as the critical and destructive forces of my "negative being" were not so easily quelled. I would not easily let go of hundreds of years of working-class resentment that seemed to be the foundation of my thought and feeling patterns. This may have been good in the end, since they were the hidden fuel that Lizzie was looking for in me. The paradox of releasing all those violent energies for a lady with an economic and social background that to me stood for the worst examples of capitalist, nuclear-powered imperialism in a bourgeois house in Golders Green confounded me.

Work sometimes gave way to games, and over those first months, I learned to play squash (yet another sport then alien to the working classes). I soon relished the chance to thrash that little rubber ball from wall to wall. My partner at the Hampstead Squash Club (which had recently been acquired by one of Roy Hart's businessmen group members, Montague Crawford) was Derek Rosen. I learned from him that the game was not simply a good bash, but essentially a dance *à deux* with a partner towards whom the slightest expression of aggression was inappropriate. I grew to love this game which almost all members of the group played regularly. Several of the group, including Roy Hart, were even Club team level players.

About four months after my first singing lesson, I had the first "real" dream of my life. Excitedly I recorded it in a book I bought for the purpose. It ended:

> I leave a theatre space where I have been part of a rehearsal. A cat, who is my friend, agrees to help me find something that the performers need. The cat leads me to a slipway such as boats are launched from at the bottom of which is a large weather-proof curtain. The cat becomes a girl, and together we eventually wind up the curtain revealing a rough and stormy sea.

At about seven or eight years old, I was shocked when I was told that cats could be male and dogs female. Until then I thought that cats were the females and dogs the males of the same species. And now a cat, a feminine animal, had returned to me and knew the way to go in order to face the elements of soul. It was prophetic of times to come. Not long after came this dream: "There is a new female member of the group. We are in a meeting, and I am learning how to kiss her." When I told Hart this dream, he grew warm towards me for the first time. He said this dream coincided with the finding of my "feminine voice."

On the higher end of the masculine voice is a realm that I experienced as feminine and which sounded like a classical contralto singer. At first I was amazed by the beauty it contained and with the new way it made me feel. I began to enjoy singing in that range for its own sake, learning that it was a dimension of myself, one that could be louder or softer, stronger or weaker, yet clearly located in my chest. It made me feel I was entering a realm I had long forgotten, for which the name "feminine" seemed right. I was in fact making my first contact with what Roy Hart's late teacher, Alfred Wolfsohn, many years earlier had called "the voice of the future," a voice that could span all the different categories that classical music had devised. Conventionally there was considered to be only one category appropriate for an individual, and the separation was rigidly based on gender lines. Wolfsohn's work had involved the transcending of these categories and the "unchaining of the human voice."

Dennis Pikes at seven or eight years old astride a stuffed lion on the seafront of Seaton.

Alfred Wolfsohn (center) as a German soldier in World War I.

CHAPTER THREE

ALFRED WOLFSOHN

The year is 1917. We are now somewhere at the battlefront but we don't know where. Here in this foreign country are trenches, trenches everywhere. I am living in these trenches. Every now and then the darkness of the night is lit up by lights, strange stars made by man. Shells burst right and left. I throw myself on the ground, my hands clawing the earth. Often someone next to me is hit. Each time I am astonished that I have been spared.

Heavy rain has turned the trenches into muddy swamps. Once I sink down in a trench, I sink into the mud. My comrades, like phantoms in the darkness, pass me by and do not help me. I am stuck in the morass and I am alone. Everything depends on my army boots, they have become my greatest enemy, for they hinder me in every movement. I rip open the sides of my boots with my bayonet and begin to crawl on all fours.

Barrage all around me. The guns from which it is coming are served by 4 or 5 Frenchmen. I don't know where they come from, I don't know who they are. They don't even know they could easily kill me. They have to keep a certain stretch of ground under fire. It is no good shouting; "Jean-Baptiste, Maurice, Pierre. I have done you no wrong; what do you want from me?" I keep crawling.

The hours pass. The firing is getting stronger and my peril greater. I pray to God but he doesn't help me. From somewhere I hear a voice incessantly calling; "Help! Comrade. Help! Comrade." I close my eyes, shaking with terror, thinking, "How can a voice utter such a sound?"' I fought a terrible struggle with myself: should I try to crawl to him or not? I did not.

Grenades whistle, a voice implores, I curse God, I hear his scornful laughter in infinite space, the earth is ripped open, the sky is a fiendish backdrop, realm between being alive—only just—and dying. What continues are the automatic movements of my body, that is all; and the unceasing questions: "WHY? FOR WHAT?"[1]

After an agony of more than twenty hours I reached a reserve dugout. I do not remember what happened after that, except that I learned later I had been hit and buried by a shell and that I awoke the next morning in the cellar of a house in St. Quentin, amongst a heap of corpses.[2]

This was Alfred Wolfsohn's account of his descent into hell at twenty-one years of age. It was in this twentieth-century inferno that his unique work on the human voice began. As he later wrote in his unpublished 1958 manuscript, *The Problems of Limitations*, "…for me it was of the utmost importance to the development of my concept of the human voice, and which at the same time led to the realisation of that concept."

The experience of the war, his subsequent illness, and eventual recovery through his particular way of using the voice were what evolved into a lifetime's research. It is known that Wolfsohn began his revolutionary approach to the art of singing in the late 20s in Berlin. And in the 50s in London, as the pioneer of the idea that the voice is the mirror of soul, he attracted international recognition with the vocal achievements of his students. It was there that he died in 1962.

But who was Alfred Wolfsohn? What were these achievements, and how do they relate to the contemporary search for soul? What did he mean by the "voice of the future?" Although I did not know Alfred Wolfsohn personally, over the years of working with his legacy through Roy Hart, it felt as if I did. And reading Marita Günther's translations of his unpublished manuscripts drew me closer to the

---

[1] From *Orpheus, oder der Weg zu einer Maske* [*Orpheus, or the Way to a Mask*]. Unpublished manusprcipt written around 1938 in Berlin. English translation by Marita Günther.

[2] From *The Problems of Limitations*, unpublished manuscript, 1958.

man and his time.[3] Eventually, it seemed to me as if his experience of Hell imposed on him from the world seemed to echo my own hell, which came from within. As I learned more about him, it was as if there was a thread that linked Wolfsohn and me through time, a thread that led to finding voice. Wolfsohn wrote in his unpublished article, *The Problem of Limitations*:

> Spiritually I was a tramp, the scapegoat of my time, the outsider, the rebel against order; I did not know whence I came and whither I went; I disguised my grief by clowning. I was always the underdog and when I did not want to believe it, I heard and saw it written again and again in black and white that I did not belong to the human race. There was one saving grace; I was not a success and I did not gain capital from those investments.

Wolfsohn possessed an inquiring and often inspired mind. Not only did he question the existence of God, he questioned the relevance of art, classical mythology, and himself. He wrote on paintings and artists, music and composers, operas and singers, cinema, contemporary writers, and classics in literature and philosophy. Wolfsohn often contemplated the nature of soul and its relationship to the body, music, and voice. It was these ideas that became a foundation for his belief in the healing powers of music, singing, and the voice. He also analysed the role he played as a teacher, which he often illustrated with "case-studies" and its parallels to and differences from the artist, the lover, and the psychotherapist.

In the Beginning

Alfred Wolfsohn was born in Berlin into a Russian Jewish family in 1896. His father had fought in the Franco-Prussian War and was proud of it. Wolfsohn wrote about his father's experience in his 1947 book, *The Bridge*, saying that, "The 1870-71 war was the climax

[3] The unpublished manuscripts include: *Orpheus, oder der Weg zu einer Maske* [*Orpheus, or the Way to a Mask*], Berlin, 1938; *Die Brücke* [*The Bridge*], London, 1947; *The Problems of Limitations*, London, 1958. They are held in the Leo Baeck Centre at the Berlin Jewish Museum. Copies of *Orpheus, oder der Weg zu einer Maske* and *Die Brücke* are also in the Joods Historisch Museum, Amsterdam. Copies and translations of these works are in the Roy Hart Theatre Archives, Malérargues, Thoiras, Anduze, France.

of his life. I had been overfed with stories about it and, being of a somewhat different nature, it must have upset my stomach. On the other hand, there was something which my father impressed upon me which stuck forever: I should always try to prove that the prejudices against Jews are unjustified." Wolfsohn's father later earned a living as a cabinet maker and died from "overwork" when Wolfsohn was just ten years old.

Wolfsohn, adored and spoiled by his mother, had two sisters and a half-brother and was sent to a good school, although he suffered bullying and ridicule there as a Jew. Alfred chose not to fight back, and the experience of being on the outside seemed to reinforce his introspective and philosophical nature. Instead of resenting his position in society, he considered being an outcast his lot in life: "I have learnt to regard this fate as my best and hardest school," he wrote in *The Bridge*, "to look upon the ever-recurring experience not as an excuse for self-pity but as a spur towards the education and development of myself as an individual."

At six Wolfsohn began to learn the violin and the piano, and later as a teenager, he sang in a quartet at Jewish festivals. In *Orpheus, or the Way to a Mask*, Wolfsohn mentions several times that as a boy he loved music and had ambitions to study and play it. He also wrote that as a choirboy he went into the Brandenburg forest to sing, an experience that revealed his identification with music-making:

> ...and his little soul, usually so lonely and withdrawn, rose upwards.... This little boy, however, did not lack courage. He played football with equal fervour even if the ball was made out of the breakfast wrapping paper. But one thing he knew very clearly: there was a difference for him whether he played football or whether he sang. When the game was finished, he was exhausted, he felt hungry and empty. But when he had sung, he was fully there, fulfilled, the music lived on in him, forced him to go adreaming about unknown and far-distant lands and sometimes it made him cry.

Then came the First World War, and at eighteen Wolfsohn was conscripted into the German army. During the war he was wounded in

the Third Battle of Arras,[4] contracted tuberculosis, and was later sent
to a sanatorium. But tuberculosis was not the only effect of the war
on Wolfsohn's health. He also suffered for many years afterwards
from what was then called "shell-shock," a term he resented. He
wrote about his objections to the term in *Orpheus* where he recounts
a discussion he had with a psychiatrist in the sanatorium: "Do you
call it an illness when a man is tortured physically and psychically, not
just for a little while but for four years, and who in response rages
and screams and falls into convulsions?"

However, Wolfsohn acknowledged in *Limitations* that his condition,
which would now be diagnosed as "post traumatic shock syndrome,"
was an illness, albeit one of the soul:

> I fell ill, broken in body and spirit. The main symptoms of
> my illness were fits which began by my hearing the voices of
> my fellow soldiers becoming louder and louder until I could
> bear it no longer and lost consciousness.

Although the visions persisted, it was the guilt of having seen others
suffer and of having denied help to the dying soldiers in the trenches
that troubled him the most. In *Limitations* Wolfsohn wrote that it was
not the psychiatrists at the sanatorium that helped him through his
illness but rather his love for singing:

---

[4] Wolfsohn did not give many clues as to his geographical movements or duties
during that war. I suggest the following from the various sources of evidence at my
disposal.

Alfred Wolfsohn was drafted into the Imperial German Army in 1914. He served as
an armed strecher bearer until his wounding and near-death experience in 1917. For the
first two years of the war (1914-16), he was stationed on the Eastern Front fighting
against Imperial Russia. With the Russian military collapsing and near defeat, he must
have been transferred to the Western Front—to Flanders, now northern France, during
the spring of 1916—as he was involved in the First Battle of the Somme from July to
November 1916.

Following minor advances made there by the Western allies, the German army
withdrew some miles to a previously prepared line of fortifications and trenches known
as the "Hindenburg Line," a position they held until November 1917. It would seem that
during April and May of 1917, Wolfsohn was in the Third Battle of Arras, where the
nightmare experiences he describes at the start of this chapter took place. This would
make sense of his awakening in a cellar in St. Quentin, a town which had remained a
few miles behind the Hindenburg Line on the German side.

> I felt that I had forfeited my claim to that which I had
> held to be the purest and highest in me: the aim to realise in
> myself the concept of a human being and therefore it
> depended on myself alone to discover the cure for my illness.
>
> The process of healing took place, without my conscious
> awareness, deep within me. My resistance to my illness must
> have grown when I began to have singing lessons…the
> unyielding presence of death which obsessed me in those
> voices was gradually overcome by the presence of a new and
> intensified life.

Although his lessons were focused on conventional forms of
singing, Wolfsohn felt his recovery began when one of his teachers
occasionally let him shout out his agony. It was through this experience
that he realized that a new way to sing was needed. He wrote in
Orpheus that he saw then the connection between using his voice and
his personal well-being:

> I am grateful to them for teaching me how not to do it and
> thus pointing out problems to me for the solution of which
> completely new ways would have to be found; ways which
> would not only be relevant to singing but to the problems
> of our human nature in general.

Wolfsohn saw that singing with the "unchained voice" was far more
than a technique using the larynx and the lungs. Instead, this new voice
needed to address the human condition and give it expression. "When I
speak of singing I do not see it as an artistic exercise," he wrote in *Orpheus*,
"but as a possibility and a means of recognising oneself, and of
transforming this recognition into conscious life."

It is known that around 1922 Wolfsohn gave up being a pupil, but
it is not clear whether he continued to work with his voice on his
own. It is likely that the tuberculosis was taking its toll and that he
suffered a lack of lung stamina. However, Wolfsohn had an important
vocal and psychological experience a short time later that came in the
form of a "meeting" with a mythological figure, Orpheus. The manuscript bearing Orpheus' name addresses at various times the reader, a
pupil, a dream figure, and at one point Wolfsohn's own death mask,
which was made for him by a sculptor friend. It is through this mask
that he arrives at the story of Orpheus as a parable for his life:

It had never been my intention to discover something new. I had enough to do trying to discover myself. I was simply forced to follow the call of a voice. Now I know; it was the voice of God I wanted to hear, the voice of God which Orpheus sang, the voice I divined as a child, of which I dreamt when I read in the Old Testament that it sounded not in the wind, not in the earthquake, not in the fire but that it was a gentle whisper. The voice of God speaks but of the soul, the soul speaks but of life, and as soul means life, God means life itself, the beginning and end of a gigantic current which flows in eternal movement, in time and space, beyond time and space, and beyond any judgement.

I had turned a deaf ear to this voice when I crawled hour after hour inch by inch, in the trenches, haunted by the horrors of hell, cursing and denying God. Somewhere, someone cried out: "Comrade, comrade!' a fellow creature, writhing in agony like me. I was terror-stricken. "You must crawl to him" my inner voice shouted—"No, you cannot, you must save yourself. Who helped you? Your comrades also passed you by" And I crawled on, was buried under rubble and awoke amongst corpses. It was then, it seems, that I lost my soul. However I have not forgotten the soldier's voice which would not leave me, penetrating me deeper and deeper, poisoning my whole being.

Since that time, I have done everything possible to find my soul again. It meant learning to affirm God whom I had denied. It meant coming to terms with the voice which would not leave me. It meant interpreting anew all that had been compressed into this one experience. It meant searching for a parable and finding Orpheus.

While having the death mask made, Wolfsohn began to sing with plaster on his face. It proved to be an exhilarating experience, and he was surprised that parts of symphonies, a violin concerto, and happy memories seemed to leap into his mind. He wrote in *Orpheus* that after the mask was removed, he relaxed and said to himself:

There are not many moments in your life which you have lived with such intensity as the one just now. Yet all you have done is to sing. If that is so, then your belief, treasured for so long, must be true: namely, that singing is

not something separate from life or juxtaposed to it, but
that singing is the expression of life itself.

"Learn to sing oh soul!" exclaimed Nietzsche, and so
now I have sung out all that which I have profoundly sensed
and felt; it was music, it was my voice which poured out of
me, not through willpower but coming from my deepest
self.

With his guilt transforming into the realization of the presence
of a divinity in the cries of the dying, his grief gave way to wonder,
and he asked himself an important question: "Why did I, who seemed
to have a promising voice, never develop as a singer?" In *Orpheus* he
wrote:

> In my work, however, I have never forgotten that I
> wanted to find the solution to my own problem. Only in
> this way could I find the answer to my question as to why I
> myself had not achieved my aim.
>
> For this reason I worked with voices however hope-
> less, because it gave me the chance to find out. I recognised
> much later that it was often exactly these apparently hope-
> less cases, i.e. singers who had studied for many years and
> come to grief over it, who allowed me to find the answers
> to my questions.
>
> I discovered that in each case it was not only their voice
> which was suffering but their soul. Experience taught me
> that no progress could be achieved if I did not succeed in
> helping to correct the psychic damage, to restore their faith
> in themselves and to transfer my own belief onto them . . .

Wolfsohn found himself in a complex role, as he thought of
himself as a singing teacher and therapist facing questions of "faith"
and "belief." Wolfsohn tells us more about the links between voice
and soul as well as about his role as a "voice-psychologist" in *Orpheus*:

> As the basis of singing is the same as that of psychic
> life, so their development proceeds accordingly in the same
> direction; the difference being that the growth of the voice is
> more distinctly perceptible than the growth of the soul. The
> psychologist can gauge the progress at hand through the devel-
> opment of the patient's dreams; the voice-psychologist likewise

can follow his pupil's dreams with his inner eye, but even more so he can hear with his inner ear all the many stages of the grounding of the voice.

In both cases, the development is brought about by coming in touch with the self, in the confrontation with the weaknesses, afflictions and imperfections of the ego. Moreover, it means a battle with the external circumstances which can either oppose or support the ego. Success and failure of the growth process, in both instances, ultimately depend on the degree of contact between teacher and pupil.

To be a teacher means to be the guardian and representative of creative life. If this development of the psychic factors of life goes well, then one says of him—on whom this gift is bestowed—that he is "called" upon and the guiding star above this "call" is "vocation." He, who is "called" upon has to obey a voice.

Although he was not initially drawn to the field, his language here is already informed by Analytical Psychology. A segment in *Limitations* reveals the influence of C. G. Jung on his thoughts:

Although for certain reasons I felt a horror of anything connected with psychology, I forced myself to read about its various systems. The more I read, the more I realised that much of the experience which I had gained from my own work ran parallel to fundamental principles of psychoanalysis and psychotherapy.

During the Hitler regime, when Jung was lecturing in Berlin for the last time [in 1938] I was naturally most anxious to meet and discuss with him the relationship between his interpretation of psychology and music. When I asked for an interview they laughed and told me that his time was too limited even for him to see all his pupils and patients. I was not to be put off by this attitude, but sent him a dream I had had about him. In the accompanying letter I said that the dream was my visiting card and also the reason for my desire for an interview.... Jung replied at once that he was expecting me at his hotel.

That the meeting, whose essential point was the relationship between Jungian psychology and music, did not fulfill its purpose, does not concern us here. What is important is that

> Jung, in contrast to [Aldous] Huxley, [with whom he was
> later in correspondence] considered the dream about himself—
> coming from a complete stranger—as sufficiently important
> to grant an interview despite the already heavy demands on
> his time.

In his effort to better understand himself, Wolfsohn adopted Jung
as a father figure, a move made evident by the ardent letters Wolfsohn
wrote to Jung after the two men met in Berlin. These letters are kept
in the C. G. Jung Archives at Zürich's Eidgenössische Technische
Hochschule (ETH) Scientific Library, and are reproduced at the end of
this volume. Although Jung's responses are passive, they show Wolfsohn's
dedication to his research. Wolfsohn believed that Jung's ideas on individuation and on the fundamental wholeness we possess at birth
could be shown in the human voice. Wolfsohn writes in *Limitations*:

> There was a period [in the late 30s], where my work was
> centred around the problem of finding the united as
> opposed to the split voice, the unity of the voice which is
> the expression of the potentially complete human being.

Wolfsohn describes in *Orpheus* hearing this unity in the human infant
and its frequent disintegration as we grow up:

> …we have all heard a baby cry. It can cry for many hours, it
> knows nothing about economy, it has no consideration for
> its throat or vocal chords. It turns red and blue but it doesn't
> get hoarse. Two tiny tender vocal chords achieve extraordi-
> nary things without suffering any harm. Why is this so?
> The baby wants nothing with its head, nothing with its will
> which is a mental function. The baby is without any inhibi-
> tions, it is possessed by one drive only: to still its hunger. It
> does not actually cry, it cries out and this represents a source
> of energy which many a singer could envy. Once its hunger
> is stilled it goes happily to sleep again with no other aim
> than to gather strength for the next screaming bout.
>   Children, on the whole also use their voices correctly,
> unless they are very inhibited, and they are not in posses-
> sion of a singing technique either. When they get older,
> they lose much of their naturalness and with it inhibitions
> set in. The grown-up has forgotten how to open his mouth in

a natural way; by adjusting himself to the world around
him, he has forgotten how to scream. And thus, after losing
this primitiveness, the voice is exposed to all sorts of defor-
mations. A voice can sound lumpy, palatal, hard and brittle
and it often sounds toneless, broken, nasal or compressed.
Behind this vocal condition lies the loss which the grown-
up suffers by not being able to preserve his state of
naturalness.

However, Wolfsohn was not advocating an early form of "primal
scream," which was "discovered" by Arthur Janov some thirty years
later. Instead, Wolfsohn's idea is that healing takes place through caring
for the full range of the voice not by isolated attention to one aspect
of it. And in spite of his reference to "losing this primitiveness," he is
talking not of a simple return to Nature, but of a return to soul
through Nature. He believed that humanity's loss of Nature is the cause
of our pain, and one's rebirth comes about through conscious vocal
expression, otherwise known as singing. He wrote in *Orpheus*:

> I live by breathing in and breathing out. I sing by trans-
> forming this breath into sound, the sound which in turn
> forms the material for the contents of the soul. Our life
> stretches from morning until evening, from dusk to dawn
> embracing the night. In the time-span of day and night, in
> the polarity of light, with all its nuances, the life of the
> human soul also vibrates. In these elements the soul rises
> and falls in equal measure between above and below, between
> light and dark.
>
> The human voice is based on the same elements. It can
> show all the colours between light and dark, it can fill the
> space between above and below in gliding through all the
> scales. Just as the day—in conscious alliance with the sun as
> generator of warmth and fecundity—can be regarded as the
> male principle and the night with its darkness and profun-
> dity as the female principle, thus, in parallel, the voice unites
> these two principles within itself.
>
> The life of the human soul fluctuates in an up and
> down movement within these two poles; flowing and
> ebbing in waves. The voice, however, represents the system
> of waves; its rhythm can change from being in a state of

> utter calm to a storm of passion, ranging in bold leaps
> from the lowest depth unto the loftiest height. In order to
> see this law operating visually, one only has to look at a
> sheet of music. The human soul, by its very nature, can
> recognise itself by its own interior space only, which makes
> it difficult to form an even approximate image of itself.

Here, Wolfsohn articulated his vision through the ancient idea of soul as a container of opposites, an idea which was also important to Jung. Wolfsohn finds a simplicity within the complexity of "conscious singing" and the "natural" voice within the singer's complexes. He continues:

> Any creative activity, and singing is one of them, has only
> one meaning, only one aim; to create expression.
> In my attempt to discover the secret of singing, nothing
> has compensated me more for all my searching and worrying
> than the discovery that that which I had one-sidedly under-
> stood as "expression" in its symbolic and spiritual sense, had
> to be taken in its literal meaning. I found that the sound of the
> human voice gained its fullest expression exactly at the point
> where the singing person—having found the right balance of
> concentration and tension—could express it bodily. Whoever
> is convinced like me that exactly the simplest things in life
> contain the most complicated problems also knows that the
> mastery thereof leads to the desired goal.

Thus the goal of the teacher of the "unchained human voice," the "voice of the future," is not only to lead students to the spiritual sources of their voices but also to its bodily roots. These roots were to become a major theme in Wolfsohn's teaching in later years as he pitted himself against the conventional wisdom which localized the source of the voice in the larynx. Wolfsohn wrote in *Orpheus* that this was a difficult lesson to teach. "Pupils came to me who knew just about all there was to know about the anatomy of the larynx, who were well informed about the mechanics of speaking and singing techniques, who could show off with clever phonetic tricks. There was only one thing they could not do: namely sing!"

However, this criticism could not be levied against one of Wolfsohn's students, Paula Lindberg, who was a well-known opera

singer in 1930s Germany. The daughter of a cantor, she was introduced to Wolfsohn by an old friend of hers, Dr. Kurt Singer, who
was a physician, psychiatrist, hypnotist, professor, director of the
Berlin Municipal Opera, and a much-published musicologist. Singer
was also instrumental in helping Jewish artists to find work during
the oppressive conditions of the Third Reich. Lindberg took lessons
from Wolfsohn, although she did not take them too seriously, and
provided him with other pupils, including her stepdaughter, Charlotte
Salomon.

Charlotte (who was an art student at the time) was so inspired by
Wolfsohn and the conversations they held, she created *Life or Theatre—
An Autobiographical Play,* which included text, pictures, and music.
Charlotte began writing the play in 1941 and completed it two years
later while in exile in southern France from Nazi Germany. The leading
man in *Life or Theatre* is named Daberlohn, which is Charlotte's thinly
disguised fictional name for Wolfsohn. Shy and uncertain about her
talent, Wolfsohn had encouraged and taught her that she might find
the meaning of life by sounding its depths. She undertook this task
and tried to see it through with all the courage, intelligence, and
creativity she had. In *Life or Theatre* Charlotte refers constantly to
Wolfsohn's *Orpheus* manuscript, which probably shows that she had seen
the unpublished book and had an intimate understanding of Wolfsohn.

Tragically, Charlotte was captured by the Nazis in France shortly
after completing her work.[5] She was sent to Auschwitz and mur-
dered there at the age of twenty-six. Wolfsohn, too, was targeted by
the Nazis for destruction because he was Jewish. But unlike Charlotte
he escaped from Germany to England at the last moment with the
help of a former pupil and lover, Alice Croner, who had fled to London.[6] In London he was enlisted in the British Army Pioneer Corps,
a Regiment for the least fit British soldiers and for friendly foreigners, and found himself again on active duty in northwest France (probably
in an intelligence capacity), but now opposing Germany.

---

[5] Charlotte Salomon's collection of artistic works is now housed in the Jewish
Museum in Amsterdam from where it has travelled in recent years to major exhibitions
in other cities, notably Paris, New York, and London.

[6] Wolfsohn told Alice Croner she should keep a faithful record of her dreams,
which she did until 1982. They were used for a research project at Zürich's ETH.

It was here that he met James Johnson, a chartered accountant with the soul of a poet, who became interested in Wolfsohn's work. Their meeting was ironic in that Johnson had been Wolfsohn's enemy during World War I, and it is likely that as soldiers they were fighting against each other on the Western Front. When the war was over, Wolfsohn continued his work in a small studio provided by Johnson at Golders Green in London. Johnson and his two daughters were among Wolfsohn's first pupils in England. However the end of the war was not the end of grief for Wolfsohn. While in London, he learned not only of the fate of Charlotte Salomon, but also of the murder of his beloved sister.

A few years after the War, Wolfsohn accepted Marita Günther as a student. Raised in Leipzig, Marita was a distant relation (her mother was a second cousin of Wolfsohn's), although she had never met him. She left Communist East Germany for England in 1949 because, being the daughter of a physician and university professor, she was forbidden to study at university. In Communist Germany university studies were reserved only for the children of farmers or workers. Marita worked in England as a domestic servant, met Wolfsohn in September 1949 and began lessons in 1951. In an essay titled, "The Human Voice: On Alfred Wolfsohn," Marita wrote:

> At first I only really saw his head, his lion-like black head of hair.[7] It seemed to me as if all his strength was gathered there. And then it was his eyes, the look he gave me, or rather the way he looked into my very being.
>
> This first encounter left a deep impression on me…. For the first time, in this studio, I heard how Alfred Wolfsohn worked with his pupils. At that time there were about fifteen men and women of different ages, people in jobs, amateurs mostly, who came in their spare time. A few were actors, amongst them Roy Hart, who later continued his work.
>
> What all his pupils had in common was that they could reach with their voices heights and depths that I had never heard before. They could produce within that range differ-ent colours of sound which moved me deeply. But what

---

[7] Wolfsohn wrote in *The Bridge* of his habit of keeping his hair long that it "had to do with my having to accept the idea that in every man there is not only a child but also a woman."

appealed to me more even than the virtuosity of their vocal ranges was to witness the relationship of teacher and pupil. It was the give and take on both sides, an incredible concentration and intensity emanating from both. It was the physical effort in the extreme which seemed to transform their bodies and facial expressions.

And then came the day I had my first singing lesson, i.e., the day that I too had a voice of such a nature that I knew I must follow this path! I believe we all have once in our lives a central experience which touches us so deeply in the very roots of our being, an experience where heart, soul, and mind are so equally involved that it can radiate upon our whole life. It happened to me more than thirty-five years ago.[8]

All of Wolfsohn's pupils called him Awe (pronounced Ah-Vey), being simply the German pronunciation of the two initials of his name. In an interview Marita told me about her first lesson:

It lasted about 20 minutes and I came out in absolute raptures. The conversation went something like:
M: "How have I done it? I have never sung before!"
Awe: "You've never sung before?"
M: (in a high girlish voice) "You know I've never sung before"
Awe: (raising his eyebrows) " And all those talks we've had?"
That phrase still rings in my ears because I immediately understood that all the talks over a gin and tonic or a beer were also singing lessons.[9]

This was the "voice-psychologist" at work, although Wolfsohn never referred to himself as such with his pupils. He saw himself simply as a "singing teacher," and while his lessons took the outward form of a classical singing lesson, the content was far from classical. Marita wrote in "The Human Voice:"

This was a "far cry" from singing beautifully. In the beginning it was a squeaking and a squeezing, a screaming

[8] Marita Günther, "The Human Voice: On Alfred Wolfsohn," *Spring* 50 (1990): 69.
[9] From an interview with the author, 1996.

> and a peeping. And out of this developed a different kind
> of beauty of the "dared expression." Like out of the days
> of the Creation something emerged that was not only beau-
> tiful: it was authentic. And this authenticity was nurtured,
> polished, and repeated until the ear got accustomed to it; or
> let us say the ability to hear underwent an equally intensive
> training.

Wolfsohn never gave physical exercises or "warm-ups." Instead he sat at the piano with his pupil, who did not move much, at his side. Sometimes he used what was called the "bashing board," an upholstered plank of wood which would be leaned against the wall. The student would lean back on the board allowing Wolfsohn to push on certain parts of the student's torso to enhance awareness of different parts of the body during vocalization. Another way he worked, often with a group, was to seek the sounds of the four classical string instruments in the voice. Wolfsohn required the student to act as if he held the instrument in his hands. Eventually a student could sound the same note with the variation of timbre resembling those typical of the violin, viola, cello, or double bass. Thus the contents of Wolfsohn's lessons varied enormously and usually in relation to his judgement of the needs of a student on a particular day.

Kaya Anderson, a pupil who joined Wolfsohn in 1956, resists casting him as only a singing teacher.

> When he gave a lesson, there was drama and tension in
> it; I cannot separate his way of teaching from his way of
> looking and listening; what went over his face, his expres-
> sion, for me, that was so musical that it never crossed my
> mind to decide whether or not he was a singer. Whether he
> performed in public or not is another question. With warmth
> and great intensity he encouraged me and many others to sing
> and discover our essential artistic and human beingness.[10]

Marita Günther agreed and wrote in "The Human Voice" that:

> Wolfsohn's voice was rather quiet, and what he had to say
> was not only directed to the mind but also to that which lies
> much deeper: the receptiveness of the heart. He was a strict

---

[10] From an interview with the author, 1996.

teacher; he had no favourites. He believed in punctuality and objectivity where the work was concerned. And at the same time he had a great sense of humour. I don't know whether this was the famous Berlin sense of humour; in any case, it had something to do with a sense of proportion, that one did not take oneself too seriously.

Another perspective on Wolfsohn's teaching comes from Sheila Braggins, who had been a pupil beginning in 1949 and said:

> An extraordinary aspect of working with Awe was the way he watched for musicality in expressions of oneself in everyday activities, the way you picked up a cup, the way you entered or left a room; every move you made was significant. It built up a self-awareness, a way to get to the centre of what one was and what one had to offer. The whole of life with him was an intense awareness; even when playing a game of cribbage! In the later years we were so deeply involved with his illness, with him as a man. We were giving and receiving from him on a daily basis and singing lessons were an extra gem; if he was well enough, if there was time. It is difficult to make this understood; the whole of life was a singing lesson. Yet done with humour and lightness. I'd learn as much about myself playing patience or cribbage with him as in a lesson because he'd often connect with a lesson you'd had with him previously. He never took a break. You did trust everything he said; you knew there were no ulterior motives; He taught many of his pupils free of charge; money did not really come into it.[11]

Wolfsohn was clearly not teaching for the money, an attitude confirmed by Avis Cole, another young student who said that he based his charges on what she could afford and that she received far more time, at less cost, than with any of her previous teachers.

Although he was not providing professional training for singers, Wolfsohn had several students with professional aspirations, including the writer Rabbi Lionel Blue and Emannuel Klein, a cantor and teacher

---

[11] From an interview with the author, 1996. Braggins, together with Günther, Anderson, and Hart, was one of the core of long-term students in daily contact with Wolfsohn. She subsequently left the work in 1964 in order to raise a family with her husband, Colin. She is now a lecturer, practitioner on back problems, and author of *The Back—Functions, Malfunctions and Care* (London: Mosby, 1994).

of Jewish religion. Avis Cole had also begun training as a professional soprano at seventeen, but she came to Wolfsohn around 1950
after four different teachers left her feeling that something essential
was lacking in her singing. She felt that Wolfsohn took her beyond
classical singing to the roots of music.

> Wolfsohn told me not to practice any more outside the
> lessons with him and, in fact, not to sing at all unless it was
> a spontaneous action. I was very happy at this time and
> now I know why; for the first time in my life somebody
> tried to understand my connection with music. My previous
> teachers had superimposed their ideas on me without seeing
> me at all, whereas Wolfsohn tried with each lesson to seek
> out what I really wanted with singing. He tried to find out
> why it was important to me and what I really had in me to
> give. And what a task he undertook! I spent the first two
> years unlearning all the bad habits I had been so carefully
> trained into…. I "produced" my voice…. I added the "expres-
> sion" afterwards.

Cole tells how she and several other students would meet to sing
songs for each other at the large home of Ina Farnwell, a well-known
piano teacher in Barnet, allowing them to follow developments in
each others' voices. These meetings seemed to foster healthy competition and mutual support. Jenny Johnson, one of James Johnson's
daughters, became Wolfsohn's star pupil because he felt she was the
realisation of Wolfsohn's "voice of the future." Cole writes in her
unpublished "An Account of Experiences with Wolfsohn:"

> …after a few years Jenny had far outstripped me in develop-
> ing the deep tones of her voice and the very high range. As
> her voice progressed, these new sounds, which started some-
> times in a rather ugly way, became very beautiful. It was
> further confirmation for me of what could be achieved….

And when Jenny Johnson first reached a certain high note in her tenor
register, Marita was thrilled:

> I was working in the kitchen and could hear that something
> special was happening through the ceiling. It was a top D.
> On a crescendo Jenny, as a tenor could easily get the top C

that singers like Caruso gave their life for. Afterwards it was
celebrated and eventually she went 3 or 4 notes above it, in a
real tenor quality.

Wolfsohn's ideas evolved according to the willingness and ability of
his pupils to respond. But it was the Johnson sisters and another student,
Roy Hart, who played central roles in opening up new territory.

In 1956 the results of Wolfsohn's new techniques were presented
on an LP recording called *Vox Humana—Alfred Wolfsohn's Experiments
in Extension of Human Vocal Range*.[12] This recording contains material
which can only be described as astounding; a twelve year old boy
demonstrating a range of six octaves; male and female voices
convincingly producing the timbres of flute, violin, viola, cello and
double basses over wide ranges; a string quartet sung by four females
voices; voices that seem to overreach the piano at both ends. The
songs sung in ranges of more than four octaves by Jenny Johnson
are most impressive. An article written by psychotherapist Eric Weiser
entitled, "The Unchained Voice," appeared in the Swiss weekly, *Die
Weltwoche*. It described what she was like on stage:[13]

> With a voice as clear as a bell, she sang the highest and
> lowest notes the piano could produce. The piano with its
> seven octaves fell silent, since Jenny Johnson's voice had a
> range of between eight and nine octaves. The impossibly
> high notes of a coloratura soprano, which can only be
> compared with the song of the nightingale, then rang out
> unaccompanied—the next minute we were treated to a full,
> deep male voice.

Roy Hart

It was about this time that another young student of Wolfsohn's,
Roy Hart, began to garner attention. In an article in the Birmingham
Post printed in October of 1955 entitled, "The Utopian Voice," Hart's

---

[12] Originally released by Folkways Records and now available on CD from the
Center for Folklife Programs and Cultural Studies, 955 L'Enfant Plaza 2600, Smithsonian
Institution, Washington, D.C. 20560 USA. Series No: 06123. www.folkways.si.edu

[13] There is no clear date indication of the year, but the weekly must have been
published in 1955 or 1956; RHTA Malérargues.

recitation of T. S. Eliot was described as "disturbing."

> Mr. Wolfsohn's claim to have extended not only the range
> but also the dynamics, colours and expressivity of the human
> voice, in speaking as well as singing, was immediately justified.
>
> … [F]ar more remarkable were Mr. Hart's uninhibitedly
> dramatic and multi-voiced recitations of T. S. Eliot's
> "Rhapsody on a Windy Night" and "In the Beginning" from
> *The Rock*. I hope there were some Schonbergians in the audi-
> ence for the *Sprechstimme* of Pierrot Lunaire was knocked right
> out of the picture.
>
> I shall write more about last night's disturbing experience
> when it has "sunk in." That may take quite a long time.

It was Hart and the Johnson sisters that helped move Wolfsohn
far beyond his Berlin period. Marita Günther, who watched Wolfsohn's

Roy Hart in Tralfalgar Square,
London, whilst a student of
RADA. 1947.

development, believed that his new students were responsible for the
change and saw a new man in Wolfsohn emerge: "The man we see in
the paintings of Charlotte was very different from the man I met,
both physically and in the mindscape that had opened up for him. By
the late 40s he had become an authority and just to look at him you
trembled in your boots." How Wolfsohn's work had changed after
the war is illustrated by Marita's account of a visit to Berlin in 1960
and her meeting with a former pupil of his, Frau Böhm:

> This lady had "worked" with C. G. Jung and had
> introduced his work to Wolfsohn. She had had some classical
> singing training as part of her bourgeois Jewish education. I
> had taken a copy of *Vox Humana* for her and on listening she
> was flabbergasted, even horrified. She couldn't recognise at all
> that this was the man she had worked with. It was then that I
> realised that the ideas about extending the vocal range had
> really only emerged in London. She had never heard a woman
> singing in the male range and vice versa.[14]
>
> In the fifties, new territory in the realm of sound was
> discovered. One must remember that at that time one hardly
> spoke of the range of a voice. It was generally understood
> that a baritone, for example, sings in the middle register
> between tenor and bass. It was of much greater importance
> that a voice simply had to be beautiful. A man therefore
> who also produces distinctly female sounds and a woman
> who goes down into a deep register ran the risk of venturing
> into the grotesque—at best something for a variety show.
>
> Although we understand and accept quite easily from
> the psychological aspect that in every female being there is
> also a male side, in some stronger, in some weaker, and vice
> versa, that every man possesses also female qualities, it was
> nevertheless a big step then to search for these parts in one-
> self and to express them audibly—not as a parody or a
> sensation but as a serious attempt to find these other sides
> and thus to learn more about oneself.[15]

---

[14] From an interview with the author.
[15] From "The Human Voice: Alfred Wolfsohn."

Of course, there were accusations that Wolfsohn's voice training caused his pupils physiological damage. The accusations were frequent enough to justify putting Jenny Johnson and Roy Hart through medical tests. Examinations of Jenny Johnson's voice and larynx were performed by Professor Luchsinger of the Zürich Otolaryngological Clinic using X-ray, high-speed film, and a stroboscope. The tests confirmed that her voice could reach a range of five octaves and six notes and discovered no abnormalities in the anatomical structure or physiological functioning of her larynx. Luchsinger noted, however, that while her larynx appeared to be very relaxed, a high degree of "mental effort" was required for her to produce the high tones. Luchsinger also suggested that the extremely high notes, "formed in a staccato manner and sounding like pipe-notes, are edge tones, in producing which the larynx is blown upon rather like an ocarina."[16] In other words Luchsinger said the top notes of the "seven or eight octave voice" are not strictly vocal sounds because the vocal folds are not vibrating.

Dr. F. Winckel of the Technical University of Berlin similarly examined Roy Hart and not only found no reason to discredit Wolfsohn's techniques of voice production but he became an advocate of his method, going so far as to say it should become a standard training method. Others outside Wolfsohn's group grew enthusiastic about his work. Biologist Julian Huxley and his brother Aldous wrote of their belief that Wolfsohn's work was of importance to both evolutionary science and to psychology. Additional support came in the form of numerous articles in newspapers and journals and through a television broadcast and radio programs in Germany and Switzerland. Wolfsohn also received glowing testimony from Dr. Paul Moses, Associate Clinical Professor in charge of the speech and voice section of the Division of Otolaryngology at the Stanford University School of Medicine in San Francisco and author of *The Voice of Neurosis*:

> [Wolfsohn is] one of the greatest experts on the prob-
> lems of the human voice in the world. His achievements do
> not only cover the teaching of singing but go far beyond

---

[16] R. Luchsinger and C. L. Dubois, "Phonetische und stroboskopische Untersuchungen an einem Stimmphänomen," *Folia Phoniatrica*, 8, no. 4 (1956): 201-10.

this: they encompass entirely new areas of expression and communication. Mr. Wolfsohn has been able to prove his theories through practical results of his teaching: to me and to many other scientists in the field of vocal expression there is no doubt that it will be absolutely necessary that his work continue since most valuable discoveries have been made by him and should be expected from him if he is able to go on. His work should be known to singers and to singing teachers, but just as much to laryngologists, psychiatrists and psychologists. In my own teaching I quote Mr. Wolfsohn's discoveries constantly and do as much from an anthropological point of view.[17]

On one level, Wolfsohn did view himself as a working scientist. He was testing hypotheses and formulating ideas, seeking to realize them audibly and have the results measured, thus publicly verified and acknowledged. This spirit of science not only brought the recognition of Dr. Moses, it led him to psychology. From the early days in Berlin, Wolfsohn's research was influenced by Jung's writing. Taking a cue from Jung and Analytical Psychology, Wolfsohn believed the voice to be "first and foremost the direct expression of the soul." The "scientific" reading of this phrase led to what seems to have been a main concern in Wolfsohn's London period—the extension of the human vocal range and its description in terms of the number of octaves, in the belief that such growth must automatically imply growth of the soul or psyche.[18] Given the spirit of the times, Wolfsohn felt it was necessary to build a scientific basis under his work in order for it, and him, to be taken seriously. Yet the exaggeration implicit in the expression "eight octave voice" was not scientific, and the examination by Professor Luchsinger had not confirmed its existence.[19]

---

[17] Paul J. Moses, letter to Alfred Wolfsohn, 16 April 1961, RHT Archives.

[18] The notes accompanying *Vox Humana* claim one voice, that of Thomas Faraday, as covering nine octaves, and references to "the eight octave voice" were often made during the time I spent with Roy Hart.

[19] Luchsinger's findings were questioned by Dr. Henry Cowell in the leaflet accompanying *Vox Humana*. [*op.cit.*] "The fact that this group does not always do exactly what they claim to do…is perhaps beside the point. The pitches that are actually sung are low, but not the extreme lows actually claimed…the extreme highs are there, in clear, pure, in-tune tones…."

In reality the student most proficient at Wolfsohn's technique had been shown to sing five octaves and six tones. While this was significantly less than was sometimes claimed, it was a vocal range that far exceeded recognized limits. And in the 50s, when the Western world seemed to be testing its limits with feats including climbing Mount Everest and running the four-minute mile, the voices of Jenny Johnson, Roy Hart, and Marita Günther were cited for years in the Guinness Book of World Records.

Wolfsohn and Jung

It is clear that Wolfsohn's idea of development of voice paralleled that of Jung's process of individuation. But for Wolfsohn, the process entailed evoking a "nine octave natural" voice that has been repressed by unnatural limitations placed on the typical vocal range.

> … [T]he original nature of the voice which originally had a range of about nine octaves and has shrunk through neglect. The separate categories of male/female and child and adult voices is against nature, and we each contain a huge potential within us but it is reduced to a much smaller version held in the larynx.[20]

Wolfsohn blamed Western culture for the loss of vocal range, claiming that it had stultifying effects on the soul. Wolfsohn's development of this idea coincided with Jung's concern, "…that Western culture in general, and Christianity in particular, have ignored two elements which are vital to wholeness: the feminine and evil or man's destructiveness."[21]

Wolfsohn incorporated into his work Jung's use of the terms anima and animus and the "shadow," and identified archetypes to help interpret dreams. But what became a form of Jungian dream analysis in London was not new to Wolfsohn. Since the 30s his pupils were encouraged to write down and discuss their dreams, and he found that changes occurring in the voice were reflected in pupils' dreams and vice versa. Avis Cole wrote about parallels between the contents of her dreams and

---

[20] *Der Spiegel*, Hamburg, 1 January 1958.

[21] Andrew Samuels, B. Shorter, and F. Plant, *A Critical Dictionary of Jungian Analysis* (London: Routledge & Kegan Paul, 1986) 160.

what was happening in lessons and how Wolfsohn studied these parallels to inform him where the lessons should lead them:

> From attending to my dreams I discovered that they had a most intimate connection with my lessons. W. used to read my dreams before the lesson started, and I think he always had a pretty good idea what to expect from me each time.
>
> Over time it seems that every aspect of my life and problems threw itself up in some way or another in this dream form. Not that we indulged in a lengthy analysis of all these things, but I learned that my mind was one whole, waking or sleeping, and to see that the same hindrances in the psyche appeared in the voice and vice versa.
>
> For me the strongest proof of this fact is, that now, looking back with these problems at least partly solved, I can see how my dream life has changed. A nightmare is now a very rare occurrence, and the state of being lost, the grief for my dog and the terrible power machine figures have not appeared for years.
>
> The voice has changed too, and when I sing now I feel clearly how I am myself a sort of power-machine and how, when I hold the right tension in my body, singing is no strain at all.[22]

Since Wolfsohn considered the voice to be the direct expression of the soul, he viewed "its growth [to be] more distinctly perceptible than the growth of the soul." Thus Wolfsohn saw that his voice work offered psychotherapy a more dynamic and comprehensive way of diagnosis than some of its existing techniques, which up until then were operating only in the visual and verbal realms, and he looked to modern music to prove his point.

> To compress all this into a formula: to reach the goal that psychotherapy has set itself to cure and educate the sick man by way of self-knowledge—it is of the utmost importance to include not only the visual and visible but also the audible. Self-knowledge requires gaining *insight*, which must include listening to oneself. Freud discovered a whole world of unconscious content in slips of the tongue. Jung, in his

---

[22] Avis Cole, "Writings on Wolfsohn as a Teacher," RHT Archives, Maléraragues.

investigation of the association of ideas, needed to perceive only a fractional retardation of the vocal reaction to gain an insight into the "complex" of the person under observation. How much more then is it possible to draw the most important conclusions from the range of the voice, its various breaks, limitations and repressions, the failure in its capacity for modulation, not to mention lack in the ability of expression of spiritual values and contents as are found in so many examples of music.[23]

To help illustrate his ideas, Wolfsohn refers to a pupil who had previously been a patient in Jungian analysis. This pupil had discovered that the deep, inner place in which she found her voice during a lesson with Wolfsohn was also the source of images she had experienced during a Jungian "active imagination" session. She wrote, "As time went on, I realised more and more that the road taken in the development of my voice was similar to that taken in following the psychology of Jung."[24]

Wolfsohn first imagined—and then gradually revealed—that we do not have only one voice or just one register in which to sound out our soul. All the categories of the classical voice, from bass to soprano, are ours if we are willing to seek them. Wolfsohn saw and heard archetypal images as "specialised voices" and worked to find their counterparts in the four basic human voices, each representing a primal image. He wrote in *Orpheus*:

> The prototype behind the bass voice is the archetype of the father, varying from the king to the priest to the drunkard…. An analysis of the alto voice shows with equal clarity that it is based on the archetype of the Manna personality, the Great Mother, belonging to the element of demonism and sorcery. The soprano represents the archetype of the anima figure with all its variations of man's idea of woman, made visible on the opera stage, The baritone and tenor embody the archetype of the animus figure, whereby the difference between the two voices is one of degree.

[23] Alfred Wolfsohn, "Notes on Orpheus," trans. Marita Günther, *Spring* 50 (1990): 77-79.

[24] *Ibid.*

Wolfsohn believed these specialised voices were representations of archetypal images, not just direct expressions of them.

But the classical voice, originating within a certain religious and aesthetic perspective and bound up with the technological developments in the world of musical instruments, was not devoid of significance. For Wolfsohn it, too, represented an archetype. Wolfsohn was the first to discern that the classical voice, as beautiful as it could be, also had its shadow—aspects that come through the spaces between, behind, around, and beyond the stylised voices of opera or other classical singing. These shadow voices often sounded shocking, alien, or grotesque, and it took a re-education of the ears and mind to hear them as part of the voice. By Jung's definition "the shadow is the thing a person has no wish to be,"[25] and through the intentionally employed voice, Wolfsohn discovered that one could enter this darker realm. Unlike Jung's visual and verbal representations of his journey into the darkness, Wolfsohn's approach implied a more dynamic relationship with the shadow. Wolfsohn wrote in *Orpheus* that he saw that relationship with the shadow becoming a functional and playful one, where "art will no longer be regarded from the purely aesthetic standpoint; it will become increasingly clear that art is life."

Wolfsohn used his ability to access the darker side to help his pupils immerse themselves in theatrical roles. When Wolfsohn worked with Roy Hart on the role of Shakespeare's *Othello*, he began by provoking Hart with personal insults until he was "really" angry. Wolfsohn then directed Hart to channel that emotional energy, giving voice not to his own rage but to that of Othello.[26] Thus, rather than being taken over by the archetypal power of anger, he could give voice to Othello as a cultural representation of the archetype of murderous jealousy. The kind of inner closeness, and at the same time the distancing this approach requires, is essentially the representation of things from the unconscious through the ear. By enabling these voices to be heard in detachment, Wolfsohn foresaw a new form of psychological integration, one in which the birth of the artist in each human being was at the centre of the process. "Everyone has the

[25] C. G. Jung, *CW 16*, § 470.
[26] This event was a breakthrough in Hart's early relationship with Wolfsohn and is recounted in more detail in the next chapter.

same possibilities to sing with a five to six octave range. There is no difference of kind but only of degree. It all depends how far the artistic gifts can be developed."[27]

For Wolfsohn, development of artistic gifts depended on learning how to bridge the male/female divide. Jung's idea of *anima* and *animus*—which, simply put, for a man is the hidden feminine side and for a woman the hidden masculine side—became a central theme of Wolfsohn's work. He observed that the voice did not diminish from physiological causes alone, and that similarly, its enlargement required more than physiological barrier breaking. There also had to be an imaginative leap—that is to say, the soul also had to be involved. Initially, in order for a man to reach into the hidden upper regions of his voice, he must imagine its emergence out of the "female" body from which it emanates. Similarly, a woman must connect to the "male" body to reveal her baritone and bass voices. But both leaps require an artist's detachment and discipline.

Like Jung, Wolfsohn believed that the *anima* and *animus* are archetypal and are thereby linked to cultural representations such as Aphrodite, Mary, Beatrice, Hermes, Hercules, and Romeo, in addition to well-known dramatic and operatic characters. Wolfsohn encouraged his more experienced students to integrate the extension of their vocal ranges into existing artistic forms, such as arias, songs, or poems. This was achieved, for example, by Jenny Johnson on *Vox Humana* and Roy Hart who performed a poem by T. S. Eliot in Birmingham in 1955. Putting the extra octaves and new vocal colours into such frames required his students to make imaginative leaps balanced by technical control; the overriding concern of the "specialised" classical singer or conventional actor. It was this technical control that gave the students a reference for assessing their own artistic achievement.

Wolfsohn had long dreamed of his students' voices being used in new forms of musical expression, and in 1956, his dream came true. Wayland Young, who wrote an article entitled, "A New Kind of

---

[27] From BBC TV, "In Town Tonight: Alfred Wolfsohn at Golders Green," hosted by Fyffe Robertson, produced and broadcast by the BBC circa 1955. The original film no longer exists, but a copy transferred onto video does. RHTA, Malérargues.

Voice" in *The Observer* on February 2, 1956, challenged musicians to use Wolfsohn's singers in their compositions. "How long will the composers take to master this tremendous new raw material?" he chided. A response came quickly from the highbrow comedian and musician, Gerard Hoffnung, who organised a humorous music festival at the Royal Festival Hall in November that same year. Hoffnung scheduled Jenny Johnson, who sang a piece called *The Lift Girl* which was especially written for her voice by Donald Swan. Reviewers swooned. The November 14, 1956 edition of the *Evening Standard* carried a review which hailed Johnson's talents and striking looks: "Pretty Jenny Johnson captivated with a voice that shot down to a man's range as well as up above an ordinary soprano's." *The Gramophone* gushed of "an aria written for a truly remarkable (and very attractive) 'bass coloratura' who had to be heard and even then could not be believed."

But some reviewers were obviously at a loss as how to receive the unusual talents of Wolfsohn's students. One demonstration earned vocal criticism when writer Arthur Koestler, suspecting that Wolfsohn must be using dubious methods, loudly exclaimed, "It's black magic!"

Wolfsohn's psychological tactics also continued to raise questions, especially where the well-being of his young students was concerned. "The psychic relationship between Wolfsohn and his students cannot easily be defined using the normal psychological terms," wrote Eric Weiser. "Suggestion and psychoanalysis undoubtedly play an important role in the release of previously hidden creative energies brought about through relaxation and the consequent mastery of mind over body."[28]

Wayland Young wondered if Wolfsohn had an unnatural control over his students, although he could see no evidence of it. "There is a perceptible element of suggestion in his teaching, and it seems that his pupils have an unusual faculty for subduing their own personalities and identifying themselves with the matter in hand," he wrote. "But there is no trace of hypnotism or of a sterile domination of teacher over pupil. Mr. Wolfsohn is an open-minded, modest man."[29]

---

[28] From "The Unchained Voice," *Die Weltwoche*.

[29] From "A New Kind of Voice," *The Observer*, Feb. 2, 1956.

Of course the media was interested in what the students had to say of their experiences under Wolfsohn. Most of what they had to say reflected a positive relationship between Wolfsohn and his students. When Fyffe Robertson, a BBC interviewer, asked Jenny Johnson, "What would you say is the biggest thing you've got out of this?" Johnson replied that Wolfsohn's techniques helped her personally more than professionally. "It's a belief in myself," she said. "To say that I know what I am doing is good and I've got something great inside of me. That's what I feel when I go to sing in front of a lot of people."

Wolfsohn, too, spoke with the media, using the opportunity to tell people what they were up against. In the BBC television interview, Wolfsohn blamed a fear of height and depth as the main reason for Western humanity's dramatically reduced vocal range. Wolfsohn later wrote that the fear of emotional expression, inflicted on people by the increasing demands of a culture worshipping the gods of power, reason, and money, meant emotion had become reduced to mere "sentimentality." Thus relearning to shout, cry, laugh, and scream were frequent and necessary parts of the work, prior to and concurrent with, the work on songs or poems.

I believe that what gave shouting, crying, laughing, and screaming a dimension beyond the cathartic release of pent-up emotion was the presence of the piano, the essential accompaniment to the classical voice. The use of the piano in this way seems to have been central to Wolfsohn's teaching techniques. He was not only interested in the sound of the shout, he also demanded that the shout be made on a specific note, and then another, and another, up or down to the perceived limits. Often these limits in themselves proved to be way beyond the classical categories, and in repetition a form of training entered into the work through which the voice would start to extend itself. This happened when the singer felt how the physical and psychic energy contained within the "ugly" emotional sound could be transformed into "beautiful" singing or "rich" declamation.

Wolfsohn assumed sections of vocal range where the voice resisted extension corresponded to psychic blocks, and he looked to the voices of infants to find evidence of this. Since a baby's voice is more flexible and hermaphroditic than our adult voices in their male and female versions, he thought later blockages were an effect of limitations superimposed by culture. I suggest further evidence of this is found in the ability of a child who changes country to adapt easily to the sounds of virtually any new language.

Wolfsohn did not ignore physiological differences between males and females. It is now known that while the voices of baby boys and girls are difficult to distinguish from each other at first, a boy's larynx enlarges significantly more than the girl's at the onset of puberty. This organ is viewed medically as a secondary sexual organ, being governed by the same hormonal triggers provoking changes elsewhere. Although a male gains depth to his range, this need not mean the loss of his boy's soprano, though it usually does so in the West. Historically, in the Catholic Church, the male soprano voice was retained by castrating boys before their voices could change. Yet adult males in the Peking Opera or Ladysmith Black Mombazo Choir sing convincingly in the soprano register.

Wolfsohn also believed that identification with or rebellion against parents could effect how the voice changes from infancy to adulthood, and he asked his pupils to seek the roots of their vocal limitations in their childhood. Marita Günther told me many years ago of her long struggle to find any kind of soprano voice, a problem she linked with her childhood loathing for her mother's soprano singing—a story I have since heard from several of my own students.

Wolfsohn's guiding idea was that each pupil could become consciously hermaphroditic and give birth to the psychological gender-opposite within themselves through their voice. He believed that vocal and sexual elements are inherently connected. He wrote in *Orpheus*:

> Just as in the sexual union all forces of the body are galvanised towards the one goal: to express the substance that creates new life, so we find the same concentration of all forces in singing in order to express the sound as the new life-creating substance. Just as physical and psychic forces come together to create this expression, thus that which is created i.e. the "EXPRESSION" contains not only a physical

> manifestation but also a psychic meaning. This common
> source of singing and love-making points to a law which
> marks the consequence of the creative force of the uncon-
> scious, the law of "EXPRESSION."
>
> In observing the singing person, I could see the same
> process taking place, albeit in varying degrees; the body
> movements made in order to achieve the sound were those
> that are made during love-making.

This observation may seem obvious, even banal, since we have
become accustomed to pop singers gyrating and thrusting their way
through their repertoire. But in the 30s in Germany or 50s in Britain
this gender bending could be difficult to accept. "In middle-class 50s
England one's upbringing had been very inhibiting, one needed to be
'nice,'" Sheila Braggins told me. "Male and female were very separated in their gender roles. Many of Awe's pupils had such a struggle
to let themselves go! Nowadays the gender and sexual boundaries
are less clear."

The Voice of Love

It is no wonder, then, that the relationships Wolfsohn maintained
with female students were complicated and difficult to unravel. In
her paintings Charlotte Salomon suggested that Wolfsohn was both
her lover and the lover of Paula Lindberg, her stepmother. Mary
Feldstiner in her book, *To Paint her Life*, suggests that he deceived
several women, who in turn helped him deceive others, including
Charlotte and some of his students. Feldstiner bases her beliefs on
Salomon's fiction, in spite of the fact that its characters' names were
not those of real life. But Lindberg, when interviewed in 1975, "dismissed the entire affair with a laugh and a wave of her hand."[30]

Wolfsohn did little to dispel beliefs that his relationships with
some students became very close. Wolfsohn himself wrote in *The
Bridge* about Charlotte, saying, "that it was not easy to make contact
with her. She was extraordinarily quiet and unwilling to drop her
reticence," an impression that Feldstiner found was substantiated by
others who knew her. He tells how one of Charlotte's paintings so

---

[30] Judith Herzberg, *Charlotte: Life or Theatre* (New York: Viking Press, 1981).

impressed him that he decided to try and help her to express herself and often found himself having to play the clown. He felt as if he was breathing life into an unborn soul. I believe there was more to his relationships than Feldstiner's "deception" implies. In *Orpheus* he wrote that he had a profound experience in the arms of a woman:

> Once I embraced a woman for a long time…then I looked into her eyes. This is dangerous when at the same time embracing someone. I discovered that my face was mirrored in the eyes of my opposite. It gave me a very deep shock; I felt an inner catastrophe.
>
> From this moment on a complete change in my relationships to another person took place. I gradually discovered that all my feelings had been based on my wish to find the unlived parts of my being in that other person. I wanted to complete the half circle which I represented into a full circle. It was MY face which I had stared at!
>
> And slowly it dawned on me from whence come all our misunderstandings and all our disharmonies. From then on I tried to forget everything I thought I had learned about the concept of love.

While Wolfsohn recognised the phenomenon of projection—a term used in psychology to explain the transfer of one's emotions or feelings onto another person—it is possible that he overestimated the power of the voice to activate psychic growth and underestimated his own charisma. It is also possible that he became inflated by the power he had over some of his students, even to the extent that he saw himself as a Christ figure. While his favourite painting was of God breathing a soul into Adam by Michelangelo, Wolfsohn was probably familiar with Jung's view of Christ as not only a religious figure but also "an androgynous figure, one in whom the tension and polarity of sexual differentiation had been resolved."[31] Wolfsohn's identification with Christ was not an unconscious or unspoken aspect of his lessons. "Awe knew that he identified with Christ and, in fact, often spoke about it and analysed it. There was a very strong urge to pass on what he believed to be the right answers."[32]

---

[31] From *A Critical Dictionary of Jungian Analysis*.

[32] From an interview with Shelia Braggins with the author.

Jenny Johnson also believed herself to be his only lover. When she discovered that Wolfsohn had had another lover for many years— a lover who was not a pupil—she left in bitterness in 1959, taking one or two other pupils with her. But, according to Sheila Braggins, the actual nature of the physical contact between Johnson and Wolfsohn was irrelevant. "If they had sex together it was not because he was her lover, it was because he was giving her singing lessons.... Sexuality was the creative process; there was no part of the human being that was divorced from another part; sexuality was not the sex act, it was everything; your touch, your look, your voice, your self, your male, your female; it was the way you eat, it was absolutely everything. It is difficult to articulate this."[33]

Kaya Anderson, in a letter dated 1974, gives further insight into the way Wolfsohn used sexual contact, or at least the fantasy of it, as a teaching tool:

> Awe once said to me that I should masturbate in front of him. And this was a seed planted in me which grew into the idea of showing my sexuality openly, of a bridge between guilt, consequent distortion of what "touch" means and the real body. I never actually did masturbate in front of Awe, but that is unimportant; the idea was planted.

Alfred Wolfsohn, Avis Cole, and Marita Günther demonstrate a singing lesson for the press in London, 1954.

---

[33] From an interview with the author.

> We do not necessarily enact all that we speak of, but the
> psyche may unfold a new energy through such an idea.[34]

Some felt that Wolfsohn's sexual contact with students was above
a black-and-white view of right and wrong. Derek Gale, a psychotherapist who has integrated a version of Wolfsohn's voice work into
his practice, was a student of Emanuel Klein, a cantor who was a
pupil of Wolfsohn's and a peer of Hart's for several years. According
to Gale, Klein often emphasised Wolfsohn's enormous love for his
fellow human beings and his desire to help individuals find a reason
for living. Although himself married and a practicing Jew, Klein
believed that Wolfsohn's physical relationships with students took
place on a level that could not be morally questioned.

The fact that Wolfsohn used touch in his efforts to enlarge his
students' vocal powers may well be the expression of his belief in
Socrates' statement that there is no learning without Eros. But some
students failed to understand Wolfsohn's ability to love all of his
students, creating misunderstandings in the studio. "During a lesson
there would be a pause about half way through," Sheila Braggins
said. "I sat while he would think aloud, in deep concentration, searching
to articulate what he'd heard and felt about the work so far, about
why you had difficulty to bring out a certain sound for example. He
often spoke of other pupils, but I knew this was in the form of a
parable, addressed to me. Some misunderstood and thought they
were the precious ones laughing with him at someone else he didn't
really love... Idiotic!"[35]

Nevertheless, it is possible that Wolfsohn demanded too much
from his students and overestimated the capacity of some to read
the parables. Although Johnson's vocal range was astonishing, she
was barely out of adolescence when she began lessons with Wolfsohn.
When she left, at the age of twenty-six, could she possibly have
contained the equivalent degree of psychic growth her six octaves
of vocal range would imply according to Wolfsohn's theory? In a
letter kept in the archives at the Roy Hart Theatre Centre, one rare
piece of criticism of Wolfsohn's work refers to the seeming absence

[34] This letter is kept in the Roy Hart Theatre Archives, Malérargues, France.
[35] From an interview with the author.

of Johnson's own personality in the presence of her remarkable voice. The writer, Hermann Kleb, worked at the National Radio Station in Zürich and had been in contact with Wolfsohn. After listening to a recording of Johnson singing Schubert's setting of a Goethe poem, *Der Erlkönig,* Kleb wrote:

> ...when I listen to that song I want to hear the singer's personality evoking the three characters in the piece, but not an actual imitation of the three voices of the characters. It's not the three characters themselves I want to hear meeting [but the singer singing the song].
> ...And now, yet another question: Regarding Jenny's voice, there where its home is, it hardly sounds any more. That has really alarmed me." [36]

It is possible Kleb was simply unable to hear with "ears of the future." But given Wolfsohn's concern for the student's psyche, it is also possible that Kleb was pointing to something important. He heard Johnson's unusual and extended voices as imitations but did not hear her singing as expressive of herself. In other words, achieving a wide vocal range and variety of timbres alone may not guarantee the expression of the Jungian Self or the artistic development Wolfsohn so ardently wished for. There is no direct relationship between wide vocal expression and consciously achieved psychological balance, between the capacity to create a particular sound and the presence or absence of a particular psychological symptom or complex. And while vocal tendencies among types of psychologically "disturbed" individuals have been noted as part of their symptomology, there seems to be another ingredient necessary to psychic and artistic maturity. This ingredient is connected to the capacity to inhibit or uninhibit the spectrum of vocal expression at will according to artistic considerations. I suspect that Johnson had many of those considerations decided for her by Wolfsohn.

---

[36] From a letter from Hermann Kleb, the National Radio Station in Zürich, Switzerland, to Alfred Wolfsohn dated 18 November 1957, kept in the Roy Hart Theatre Archives, Malérargues, France. Translation by Anna Mühlemann.

Hindsight

In light of the extensive revisions and critiques that Jung's ideas have undergone, Wolfsohn's idea that "the basis of singing is the same as that of psychic life," now appears too linear. However, in its time it was an hypothesis which served as a frame for exploration, and it bore vocal fruits the like of which had never been heard before. Yet research into the application of these fruits to mature artistic performance was to require more years. It seems that Wolfsohn overestimated the role of his voice in his own hard-fought individuation process and underappreciated the other powerful factors at work in his life.

Jung believed that individuation cannot be brought about or required by the analyst. Instead, psychoanalysis simply provides a favourable environment for the process. Perhaps the same is true of the "singing lesson." The accounts of Wolfsohn's pupils suggest a tendency to try too hard to direct his lessons, and that in pursuit of showing the "voice of the future" to the world in the person of Jenny Johnson, he underestimated her need for his presence. Kaya Anderson suggested that his periods of illness in the late 50s meant that he was not always there for Johnson, neither emotionally nor physically. It is possible that Johnson's departure was necessary for her own individuation process and a further step towards embodying her enormous vocal range. In carrying his insights about singing and sexuality into action, Wolfsohn may have transgressed a rule of therapy that most people believe in today. While he theorised about being "the voice psychologist" and equated development of voice with development of psyche, Wolfsohn called himself a singing teacher. Here lies the paradox which continues in the work up to the present day. Is it therapy, education, art, religion, love, or simply life?

Although Wolfsohn remained a lone pioneer in the field of voice and psychotherapy, he did try to maintain a correspondence with Jung from the 30s into the 50s.[37] But Jung's replies consistently disappointed Wolfsohn. In reply to Wolfsohn's last letter sent to Jung early in 1955, Aniela Jaffé, Jung's secretary, wrote to say once again that

---

[37] Wolfsohn's letters to Jung are in an appendix in this new edition. The originals are to be found in the Jung archive in the ETH in Zürich.

Jung would not be able to respond personally. However, Wolfsohn's efforts to connect his theories with Jung's did not end here. Derek Rosen, who was a student of the young Roy Hart in 1958, remembers Wolfsohn sending Hart to a meeting with Jung in London. Although the date, place, and origin of the meeting have been forgotten, at an early point during the meeting, Hart referred to Jung's *anima* theory and then proceeded to demonstrate it vocally. When Hart began to sing with a feminine voice, Jung asked him to leave. Hart's interpretation was that Jung could not cope with the implications of what he had heard. Thus ended twenty years of Wolfsohn's attempts to reach Jung's ears, mind, and heart.

Every Beginning Must....

Wolfsohn died on February 5, 1962, from complications connected to his earlier tuberculosis. Even as death approached, Wolfsohn's grasp on life and his desire to teach remained strong. During his last months, when he was physically too weak to work in his studio, he

Alfred Wolfsohn and Roy Hart on the Isle of Wight, 1961.
Photo Kaya Anderson.

would teach from his bed. His students returned the favour by remaining faithful. "He was a suffering man who made something out of nothing," Marita said when she reflected upon his death. "I consider that I received an all-round education from him." Sheila Braggins, too, said that his influence on her was immense. "He came out of the disaster of war, the cruelty, the misery, the denial of humanity, and he made something beautiful out of the human cry," she said. "He gave me an immense basis for insight in looking at the world and people. My perception of my patients, and I believe my relationships in general, is grounded in that experience."

There are no universally accepted way to assess spiritual, psychological, or artistic achievements. However, it is certain that the spirit of Wolfsohn's work animated the work of Roy Hart and the group that formed in the 60s—the group I joined just five years after Wolfsohn's death. It was in that group that the themes and questions with which Wolfsohn had grappled all his life continued to be investigated and expanded.[38] Roy Hart added to Wolfsohn's musical perspective the dimension of theatre, and it is through this combination that Wolfsohn's "voice of the future" was to be realised.

---

[38] In 1966 Jerzy Grotowski, the famous Polish experimental theatre director, visited the group. Years later, in 1979, he told me of his certainty that behind "...the kind of beautiful human solidarity that was there in that group, lay the traces of very special work.... I think Wolfsohn was a very special and wise old man." From a transcript of a talk given at The First International Conference on Scientific Aspects of Theatre, Karpacz, Poland, 1979. *Roy Hart Theatre Journal*, Malérargues, France, 12 April 1980.

Roy Hart (with Paul Silber) during a rehearsal of *Mariage de Lux*, 1973.

CHAPTER FOUR
Roy Hart Takes Over

By 1969 Roy Hart had taken Alfred Wolfsohn's work beyond the London studio and into the international spotlight. He accomplished this by expanding Wolfsohn's vision and deepening the dimension of theatre to Wolfsohn's singing techniques. But Hart, who was Wolfsohn's longest working and most advanced student at the time of his death, did not take over his work automatically since Wolfsohn had not designated a successor. For Roy Hart the challenge was not only to overcome his own neuroses and insecurities but to reassemble Wolfsohn's group of singers under his own aegis. Although it was not easy, the result was explosive, and in reviews that appeared in 1969, Hart emerged as a powerful, memorable, yet disturbing performer. Comments on the *Eight Songs for a Mad King* by Peter Maxwell Davies noted Hart's ability to use voice to convey a psychological state:

> ...of all the new works given in 1969 quite the most memorable has been the *Eight Songs for a Mad King* of Peter Maxwell Davies.... This is disturbing music, deliberately so with the all-too-graphic representation of George III in his madness.... Roy Hart represents the king, using his as yet unique vocalisation of two and three notes at a time, harmonics and every imaginable squeak.
>
> —Edward Greenfield, a noted critic of *The Guardian*

> ... Roy Hart, the singing actor is an artist who commands all the voices of the human registers...added to which he gives an acting performance which stretches from the most tender allusion to the most macabre realism. All this was simply phenomenal, unique, sensational. Yet it lay beyond all

"sensation." It was so deeply stamped by immediate experience; it was the art of presentation which at every minute used the means available in a conscious way, and yet never transgressed the borderline that leads to trash.

—Joachim Heinz of *Die Welt*

Sung over a compass of some five octaves with astonishing virtuosity by that extraordinary performer, Roy Hart. It is difficult to imagine that the work could have any other protagonist.   —Desmonde Shawe-Taylor of *The Sunday Times*

Reviews of Hart's performance of *Versuch Über Schweine* by Hans Werner Henze showed that Hart's vocal range could stun an audience:

… Nightmarish heightened speech ranging from gruff low-pitched syllables to high falsetto vigorously declaimed and backed by a variously ominous and raucous orchestra that brought the work to a tense, frightening climax. —*Daily Mail*

… It was an uninhibited, confident, astonishing performance—and perhaps a little hard to take…. —*The Financial Times*

It is a parody, a caricature, ferocious even, in the manner of a Grünewald painting, or late-night hysterical oratories of a Hitler. One found oneself plunged, with shivers in one's spine, into a world of horror, from which we have barely emerged. All the modern gimmicks—of which we sometimes get examples which seem to be founded on nothing—here take on their true meaning…. It was haunting and Mr. Hart made a great success of it…. —*Feuille d'Avis de Laussanne*

Performances of Euripides' *The Bacchae* by Hart's group, "The Roy Hart Speakers/Singers," were seen as a demonstration of the inner human conflict through voice:

A magical and fascinating spectacle! … The event of the festival…The text here provides the basis for sounds, movement and expression which translate the struggle between conscious and unconscious, in each character, in each actor and finally—and this is the marvel—in each spectator….

In truth the play is not played; it is lived by human beings who integrate into their roles—which are interchangeable—

their own humanity, giving more than a performance and forcing one to react not merely as external spectators. The method does not only have psychotherapeutic value, at the limit of real and unreal, it allows one to experience a performance of which the mystery, beyond what we see and hear, dives into an unknown, which is in each of us, and which causes us disquiet.
—M. Borrelly of *L'Est Républicain*

... I nearly fell into a coma! ... An amazing mixture of (horizontal) gestures and (vertical) sounds, torsions and distortions of an unequalled suppleness from which spring sparks of a high tension current.
—C. Sarraute of *Le Monde*

It was clear that with Roy Hart, Wolfsohn's extended voice techniques and his search for scientific validation evolved into something powerful. Wolfsohn's work was transformed by Hart into performances unique in depth that touched spectators in a new way. Hart's performances demonstrated a proximity of psyche and performer, composer, and audience. In other words, Roy Hart took what Wolfsohn had begun and made it his own.

A Born Actor

Roy Hart was born Ruben Hartstein on October 30, 1926, to Polish-Lithuanian parents in South Africa. Early on he had an Orthodox Jewish education and later studied English, the history of music, philosophy, and psychology at the University of Johannesburg in Witwatersrand. At school he was given major roles in theatrical productions and it was often said, even then, that he had a beautiful voice and an innate talent for theatre. Derek Rosen knew Hart in Johannesburg and recalls that his "performance of 'Peer Gynt' was most impressive—you'd have thought he was already a professional!"

However advanced his theatrical skills were, it was difficult for Hart to make friends, and he felt conflict about being on stage; a problem that haunted him for years:

... I was always considered an odd person: that is to say, I never made friends easily; because of my lack of understanding of why things were like that, I could not establish a bridge between this fact and those who found no difficulty. In essence, I literally did not have friends.

I stayed in South Africa until I was nineteen, when the war was just about finished. All this time I knew there was something seriously wrong inside me, although no-one could figure it out, because I appeared to be completely and perfectly sane, not neurotic. There was a conflict between my innate desire to go on stage and my family, of Rabbinical origin, for whom theatre was considered blasphemy. My mother had been forbidden to take up a scholarship in drama and the same attitude was taken with me. I also had had this mental conflict, about the morality of the theatre, in relationship with the so-called morality of other activities. As a consequence I started to study medicine, considered more in line with my racial origins; but in a determined moment I decided to leave South Africa and I dropped what can be called a materialistic way of living. When I left South Africa I decided to renounce my body.[1]

While Hart's grandfather instilled in him a deep religious sense, his mother had what Hart called "the Jewish love of show business." In her letters in the early Fifties she would ask him why he was not as successful as the neighbours' boy, "Lauri," the stage and film actor Laurence Harvey. Although his religious sense and his desire to succeed in theatre seemed contradictory to him, Hart tried to keep the two impulses in harmony. It was through Hart's meeting with Wolfsohn that the combination began to work, and Hart later also met critical success. It was at the time of this meeting that he changed his name from Ruben Hartstein to Roy Hart.

When I arrived in London I was awarded a scholarship from the Royal Academy of Dramatic Arts (RADA). I met Alfred Wolfsohn almost immediately. My first meeting with him was surprising, because I suddenly realised that for the first time I was dealing with someone who could be called a human being. He did not tell or ask me the conventional phrases we all know. Later on, when I considered this phenomenon, I understood the reason; he accepted me just the way I was. When I asked him if I could work with him he answered, "We will see."

---

[1] From three interviews with Roy Hart published in *Primer Acto*, No. 130, Madrid, March, 1971.

> The important thing is that his teachings were always in
> conflict with those that I received at RADA; this conflict grew
> over the next two years since at that school I played the princi-
> pal roles. I thought I had to forget everything I had learned up
> until that moment; it appeared to me that I must abandon the
> Word, for what could be called the Sound.[2]

Hart's initiation into Wolfsohn's world came shortly after they met. Hart was having difficulty in the part of Othello, specifically in the moment where he murders Desdemona. Hart had invited Wolfsohn to dinner in his small flat in order to explain the problem: he could play it but felt false, if he were in Othello's position Hart felt he would never act that way.[3] On hearing this Wolfsohn said, "So, you are not a murderer? Please lock the door." He put aside the meal they were finishing and began to provoke and insult Hart so vehemently that Hart flew into a rage. Wolfsohn pushed him on and, neighbours notwithstanding, encouraged Hart to give voice to his new emotion: Hart felt as if he could kill Wolfsohn. Quietly Wolfsohn asked him the question once more, this time knowing the answer, "So you are not a murderer?"

In transferring this experience and its sounds to the character of Othello, Hart did not meet with the approval he may have anticipated. "All the attempts to incorporate what I was learning from Wolfsohn with what I was doing at RADA made them laugh. Although I was a good student, everybody said that I was hypnotised by a lunatic."[4] However, from this experience Hart realised how much violence was hidden in himself and felt that, like so many other actors, he was living in his head. Hart's dedication to Wolfsohn only grew and he found it necessary to make professional sacrifices to continue his study:

> Another crucial moment of my life was the time when I
> refused a major role so that I could carry on studying with
> Wolfsohn. At that time we had decided to dedicate ourselves
> to experimentation; we were going to study a play and divide it
> into parts from the point of view of vocal sounds.
>   It was then that he became ill and as I was already working
> with some students I had to start taking care of the others. In

---

[2] From *Primer Acto*.

[3] From an account by Ian Magilton in *Voice*.

[4] From *Primer Acto*.

this way I gained much experience. Thus I was separated from
the orthodox passage through RADA. The director considered
me lost. My parents thought the same thing. I then began to
work in various institutions for the mentally ill, for older
women, and for adolescents.[5]

Thus, Roy Hart made a fundamental break with professional theatre and
took another step along the way that Wolfsohn had pioneered in using
the voice as an instrument for therapy. Around 1960 Hart began working
once a week at Shenley, a psychiatric hospital in North London. He
viewed these visits as necessary research work in the cause of discovering the healing power of voice, and he maintained a connection with the
world of psychotherapy by attending several international congresses.[6]

Like Wolfsohn's lessons, the early years of Hart's group included a
strong psychotherapeutic dimension, with part of Hart's therapeutic
efforts being initially directed at his own insecurities about his skills and
his self-image. "As an artist he was vain about his looks," Marita Günther
said. "His focus on intensive exercise was due to a tendency to get fat
quickly, inherited from his mother."[7] Paul Silber, who read Hart's student
diaries, said bluntly, "Women found him ugly, and I think Roy found
himself ugly. He was certainly distressed that women seemed inclined to
distance themselves from him. Indeed, much of his quest focused on a
desire to transform himself from a frog into a prince."[8]

Hart had begun teaching under Wolfsohn, and in the 50s he led a
weekly evening group session in Wolfsohn's studio which explored the
expression of dramatic texts from Shakespeare, operatic librettos and
expressive movement to recorded music. Early members of Hart's
group included Kaya Anderson, Robert Harvey, Derek Rosen, and
Sheila Braggins. Derek recalls that Hart's way of giving group singing
lessons evolved slowly:

I was one of a row of pupils standing close to the piano. From
there Roy would work with one person for five minutes, then

---

[5] *Ibid.*

[6] August 1967 Wiesbaden; Seventh International Congress of Psychotherapy. August 1970 Zagreb; Sixth International Congress of Psychodrama. August 1972 Tokyo;
Seventh International Congress of Psychodrama.

[7] Marita Günther, from an interview with the author.

[8] From a privately printed essay by Paul Silber, "Who was Roy Hart."

the next along and so on, continuing to work on the sounds already expressed, though he might well follow something new if it emerged. The lesson gradually evolved like that, going round the circle.[9]

However, Robert Harvey, a dancer from the West End musical *The Pyjama Game*, received individual lessons from the start in a rented studio in central London. "I couldn't sing," he said. "And for musicals it was an advantage to be able to do so. But I didn't want to have conventional lessons. The psychological dimension I had heard about attracted me." To Harvey it seemed the group work emerged when Hart allowed one pupil to stay on during the lesson of another and in "the mixture of things in the singing lessons, especially dreams, which were the impulse for discovering how to live."[10]

While Wolfsohn was ill, Hart earned extra money as a house assistant in commercial theatres, and it was there that he found his first students, many of whom were dancers. According to Harvey, Hart's students did not always fare well. "There were many of them," he said. "Some left furious or disappointed after a few sessions, but though there were buckets of tears, I felt very stimulated by the end of my lessons." Wolfsohn, whose condition was declining, sat in on some of these early lessons.

Roy Hart was hesitant at first to carry on Wolfsohn's work, saying that the move was the result of "a calling" rather than a personal decision to form a group. According to Marita Günther, several long discussions with Hart revealed that his hesitation was related to his questions about Wolfsohn's use of sexuality in teaching. If Hart was going to reassemble the group, some things would change. Hart had suffered from the secretive way Wolfsohn had "experimented with Eros" while teaching and told Günther that, "although I uphold Awe, I want to be open about sexual relations."

Hart's group, which grew to about sixteen members, continued Wolfsohn's work combining voice with therapy, and in 1964, a thirty-minute documentary film of the group was made. The film gives insight into the way Hart was combining psychotherapy, drama, music, and religion. In the film Hart hints at his aspirations to create a new type of society:

[9] Derek Rosen, from an interview with the author.
[10] Robert Harvey, from an interview with the author.

> [The group's work is] a breaking down of human barriers and
> the creation of a happier, warmer society.... We believe that
> people tend to live on a monotonous and unconscious level.
> When individuals join the group we try to overcome this in a
> variety of ways. One is by deep and complete breathing.

The film then documents a group exercise called "the amoeba." It begins with Robert Harvey leaping wildly and gulping in air. He then crouches
down like a frog and expels the air quite rapidly and with tremendous
energy and intensity. He repeats this seven times. He then pulls in a
second person and, holding her arm, they go through the same seven-
fold cycle until she pulls in a third. This repeats until, as Hart says in the
film, the whole group is pulsating in "a natural rhythm based on breathing. Each individual has overcome internal deadness, and we are feeling
and acting together as a group. The rhythm culminates with the
emergence of Anna Allen when she starts to perform 'to be, or not to
be.'" In this scene Anna seems to struggle physically and emotionally, this
way and that, trying to break free from the group. They display a kind of
acting that can only be described as "non-theatrical."[11] Anna says in the
film that, "after some time in the group, I realised that I had no contact
with my body. And through using the voice, I am coming into contact
with various facets of my personality which had hitherto been hidden to
me. I didn't know anything about them."

Hart explains in the film how Anna's reaction was not unusual for
those in the group:

> Although Anna is an actress and is establishing the basis
> for a dramatic performance here, it is not performances in which
> we are primarily interested. A performance is just one manifes-
> tation of what happens as a result of this voice training....
>
> We know that everyone has a voice, not simply a speaking
> voice but a voice which is pure energy and comes from the
> whole body...in all other expressive fields what the individual
> is doing is external to himself but in this type of voice
> production he is going inward. Because of this it is an
> intensely personal experience.

---

[11] This performance was similar in power to the acted rape scene I witnessed early
in my association with Roy Hart.

This personal dimension was confirmed by everyone who worked on their voices with Hart at that time. In the film, Sylvia Young reminisces about her first lesson with Hart when she had to sing her name. "The way I was made to sing it terrified me, and I felt for the very first time as if I were two people and meeting myself for the very first time. After more lessons, when I heard all these voices, I had to be aware that this was also me, that there are aspects of my personality of which I was not aware before…." Of the individual sessions Derek Rosen said that Hart's lessons often involved physical work that left his students exhausted.

> Roy didn't force me but he would take me as deep as possible. I couldn't go very high at all. My top note was about middle C when I started. It took me years to break through that barrier. He made me work very hard physically to try and connect my voice to my body. And as my voice was so feeble, he was trying to make me do intense sounds which were also related to texts and dramatic characters. He used whatever means he could find to help connect your voice to your body.
>
> It took many years of hard, physical effort before there seemed to be any link between the effort I put into making a sound, and what actually emerged. I think I was a particular case in that way. I was extremely shy and had never sung before.
>
> He did push you very hard sometimes, but then he could also be very tender afterwards. Or if he felt you were just wallowing in sentimentality, he'd just yell at you! It varied according to the instant. There was no fixed method; he would listen to your voice, and he would go from there.[12]

Between 1963 and 1967 several visitors came to the studio to see Hart's group in action. One of them was R. D. Laing, the Scottish psychiatrist who was known for his development of "anti-psychiatry." Hart and other members of the group had been impressed by Laing's book, *The Divided Self*, which expressed ideas that seemed parallel to their own. At some point during the meeting Hart asked Laing if he could execute a hop, step, and a jump. Although he was willing, he was unable, and the session continued until Laing stood up and moved towards the door saying, "Very interesting Roy, we must meet" as he left. It was later said that he was in need of a drink and a cigarette—

---

[12] Derek Rosen, from an interview with the author.

but this may not have been true. A subsequent meeting never took place.

Another early visitor was theatre director Peter Brook who came to see Hart's group in 1966. After the visit he described the work as "full of pith and moment" and wrote, "what they are doing could certainly be of interest and value both culturally and educationally to the English theatre as a whole. There are no other groups with the same aspirations."[13] Brook returned some months later after realising that there were possibilities for nonverbal sound in his own theatre. Hart's work must have influenced Brook since his acclaimed production of Shakespeare's *A Midsummer Night's Dream* the following year contained several passages closely resembling work he had witnessed in Hart's studio.

Brook also brought Jerzy Grotowski, then a young Polish theatre director who became a key figure in the attempt to return theatre to its roots in the body and psyche of the actor. Grotowski seemed to have difficulty in acknowledging Hart as heir to Wolfsohn and, according to Rosen, "Grotowski ignored Roy altogether—he couldn't face him— and kept asking individual pupils about how Awe worked, implying Roy had deviated from Awe's path. Roy was teaching and directing us through various lesson and texts and each time we paused, Grotowski would ask a question but ignoring Roy."[14] Hart must have taken Grotowski's rejection seriously since he refused Grotowski's later invitation to the group to appear as background in a film. Hart said he would not allow the group to appear in the film "because it seemed to me that his attitude towards certain vital situations was not the same as mine."[15]

Despite problems with Grotowski, many contacts were made over the years in the fields of psychology, theatre, and music. For Hart these seemingly discordant connections made perfect sense.

> If I talked with a musician he would say that he was not a
> psychologist; if to a psychologist, that he was not a musician;
> the man of the theatre asked us what he had to do with therapy;
> and the therapist told us that he was not a man of the theatre,
> and so on. But for all of them there was a growing recognition

---

[13] Letter written by Peter Brook to the Greater London Council in support of a financial grant in 1966. Roy Hart Theatre Archives, Malérargues.

[14] Derek Rosen, from an interview with the author.

[15] From *Primer Acto*.

that the artificial separation between various disciplines is the making of a schizophrenic outlook and that it is necessary to find a bridge that unites these apparent opposites. However, although the theory invariably interested them in great measure, when they listened to the manifestation of our work they turned their backs and began to run the other way.[16]

Beautiful Singing

You never knew what might happen at Roy's "studio meetings." One Sunday session began with the floor strewn with the day's newspapers. Leslie Thompson was asked to read an article to the group, and after a few sentences, he was stopped. We were asked what we had heard. Roy would pass quickly from one reply to another until someone spoke of the way Leslie had emphasised this or that word and not another—exactly what Roy was interested in. Roy then looked into why Leslie spoke the way he had, and soon we were into Leslie's head, examining his dream world and his emerging relationship with Anna Allen. Then it was her turn to read the article. We spent much of the session developing our capacity to hear beyond the words to where the speaker put emphasis, and where not, and thereby, their psyche. Then two people were reading different articles at the same time, and they were soon directed by Roy to listen to each other more and make pauses, *crescendos, ralentandos, decrescendos*—music, in fact.

Another session resembled scenes from the 1964 film of the group, in which people were asked to perform or rehearse a poem, song, or text they had previously learned. Roy would indicate who should start, but practically before the chosen member could get up and say the first word, they were told to "sit down!" A person could make many starts before he or she displayed the authenticity or the engagement which Roy was seeking. Or they simply never got a chance to go further that day. Roy's instructions seemed to be accepted without qualms or resistances. Apart from my short experiences in the Army Cadets, it was new to me to see people seeming to behave like marionettes directed by someone else, apparently with full acceptance.

In other sessions there were powerful solo renditions, and the list of these memorable, but private performances seems endless. There was

[16] From *Primer Acto*.

Anna Allen's "To be or Not to be;" "On with the Motley" sung in a belting tenor by Lizzie; Robert's gut-wrenching "Death in the Afternoon" by Garcia Lorca; Derek Rosen's haunting voices interpreting T. S. Eliot's "The Hollow Men;" and "Molly Malone" virtually shouted by Nadine Silber in a mock-cockney accent.

There were also lighter moments. Once Roy asked me if I knew the meaning of the term *bel canto*. I guessed the meaning of the first word correctly, "beautiful," but I went astray on the second, guessing it meant "cunt." (It means "song.") My answer was met with a burst of warm laughter from Roy and the group. I like to imagine that he heard in my answer an echo of Wolfsohn's conviction that sexuality holds keys to unlocking the vocal.

In 1967 just before I joined the group, Roy and the other members had begun for the first time to work on a complete play. It was the ancient Greek tragedy of *The Bacchae* by Euripedes.[17] By the middle of 1968, rehearsals of this play became more frequent, eventually to the exclusion of the other kinds of sessions. I was required to learn certain passages of the chorus, and I was soon learning how to declaim in rhythmic unison with others lines such as:

> On, On! Run, dance, delirious, possessed!
> Dionysos comes to his own;
> Bring from the Phrygian hills to the broad streets
> of Hellas
> The god, child of a god,
> Spirit of revel and rapture, Dionysos!

As a director Roy could be demanding. Once I scratched my ear, and he shouted at me, "Dennis! Stop fidgeting!" Such moments generated a feeling of anger towards him and inadequacy about myself. This effect was deliberate. He once likened himself to Arturo Toscanini who demanded full attention from all musicians in his orchestra whether they were playing or not at a particular moment. The rehearsal atmosphere was as concentrated as that of the meetings. Roy permitted none of the messing about or breaks for a cigarette and chat that were common in professional companies at the time. Once, upon seeing a member of the

---

[17] This version of the play was translated by Philip Vellacott.

group with drooping socks, Roy lectured to the group for thirty minutes that anyone who is really ready for life will always have his socks pulled up.[18]

In retrospect it seems obvious that Roy was hard on the group because he was trying to get what he wanted from his performers. He once said that, as most of us had little self-discipline, some help from the outside was a necessary and creative thing. But at the time it was less clear to me that I had joined a theatre group. Although Roy's shift in focus away from the therapeutic to the theatrical was just beginning, it was a shift that was to become more obvious over subsequent years. Still for me, it was very much a self-development group, and with my therapeutic needs, Roy's frequent attacks were not easy to take. Given no respite from Lizzie, who at that time closely followed Roy's approach, I sometimes felt devastated, and unlike in a psychotherapeutic context, there was little tolerance of resistance.

Difficult though these efforts in awareness were, being caught in a fantasy of "consciousness development," I was able to tolerate Roy's attacks because they seemed to reflect Gurdjieff's exercises for "consciousness raising." I needed to find reasons for accepting rules and ways of doing things that the working class man in me rebelled against. For example, when a lesson entailed Lizzie pressing her fist between my teeth for several minutes as I "sang" on the notes her other hand was simultaneously playing at the piano, I could accept it. This was because I had begun to find pleasure in the increased volume and range of my voice I was discovering.

Roy's acceptance of, and focus on improvisation also appealed to me. Outside of jazz, at the time there was little acceptance of improvisation as a means of artistic expression, and anyone open to its use usually aroused my interest. My adolescent ear, which had taken delight in oddball sounds like the honk, the hoot, the burp, and the fart, was now developing to include all aspects of the voice. With Roy's teaching I learned that what lay beneath certain sounds might appear later in the recall of a dream or a moment from childhood. I saw this happening to me when one day, after working on my "feminine voice," I suddenly recalled how much I had enjoyed mocking female opera singers on the

---

[18] Richard Armstrong, from an interview with the author.

radio at the age of twenty. Now I realised I simply enjoyed singing with that part of my voice, being touched by its beauty.

One Sunday we ran through the whole of *The Bacchae* for the first time. It was presented as a dream with Dorothy Hart as the "Dreamer" surrounded by the group lying on the floor, in what the program later described as "an amoebic mass, our audible breathing indicating that we had entered the dimensions of dream." Throughout the performance her comments aimed to give psychological insight to the play and relate it to present day experience. These aims, which were enhanced by the inclusion of several disconnected solo pieces, had attempted to bring out the contemporary significance of the play. In addition, the traditional roles played by actors were jumbled. The role of Dionysos was played by three people, male and female, and Agave, the mother of Pentheus, was played by a man.

These rehearsals continued over many sessions, and the concentration demanded of us was exhausting. At times I resented Roy's role as director, sitting in his comfortable high-back chair. He usually spotted my resentment, though, and would remark on it, sometimes with "humour" which turned on the image of "Dennis" as a "clot," or a "lump of clotted cream." I wondered at those moments if he perceived something peasant-like in my nature, or if his remarks were a reference to my recent, unglamorous past.

Once, after several of these three hour run-throughs, I was surprised to feel more awake and alive than I had when the rehearsal had begun. I found that my mind was quiet, my eyes and ears were tingling, and warm feelings towards my fellow performers flooded through me, though I doubt if I was able to express them at the time. The rehearsals became a ritual for me, where time was no longer chronological but musical, dramatic, and dreamlike. Despite my previous feelings toward Roy, I began to look forward to the rehearsals as a kind of religious service. Roy said his work was intended "to aim at a unifying of body and mind, and of conscious and unconscious." I seemed to be experiencing just that. In the end, those sessions enabled me to break the chronic drug user's mentality that held me and allowed me to see that there might be other ways towards "consciousness."

Pinter Meets Hart: An Interview

R oy Hart invited Harold Pinter to attend one of these sessions, and he accepted, having been impressed by Hart's performance at the premier of *Eight Songs for a Mad King*. Pinter, an English playwright, director, and actor who won international acclaim for his play, *The Caretaker*, had also studied dramatic arts at RADA, although Hart left in 1948, the year Pinter started. The two men's experiences at RADA were similar in that Pinter had also been unimpressed with RADA's teaching and had left it early. I played squash with Pinter a couple of times during his visits to the Club, and he soon realised more than squash was happening there. In an interview in December, 1997, at his London home, Pinter remembered what it was like to meet up with the group at the Club in 1969:

> No, I didn't know Roy Hart prior to my joining.[19] I was very much on the periphery of the Abraxas Club. I had joined in order to learn squash. After a few visits I became aware that there was more than squash going on in the building. At the entrance to the changing rooms there was a flight of stairs and I would see people coming and going. I became very curious to know what is going on up there. There was another area in the club and something else was taking place there.[20] It lasted about two hours. I was a silent witness, not invited to participate. I soon discerned a palpable tension in the room. I found Hart's role very strong, a man of considerable power and I was not sure how this was being used. To put this more bluntly, I had the impression of an enormous creative intelligence, that was evident, but several of the people, or actors there seemed intimidated by him. How did he use this power? I thanked him very much and went away. There was a very singular, unusual procedure going on.... Later he invited me to go again, and

[19] Early on during this interview, I asked Pinter if he had known Hart before he joined the Club. This was not an idle question, but one based on several parallels and co-incidences that had struck me when reading a biography of Pinter written by Michael Billington. Like Hart, Pinter is also of Jewish descent, and sometimes an actor. And during his time at RADA, Pinter had been in a performance based on the poem, "The Rock," by T. S. Eliot. Hart had also performed parts of this poem in the 50s and early 60s. It was a recording of this demonstration that had been my first encounter with Hart's voice.

[20] Roy invited him to a rehearsal in the Studio, and Pinter and I established that it must have been during the period following *The Bacchae*.

take part, maybe write something for you. I didn't accept the invitation and went on playing squash.

Pinter, who acknowledged that his impressions were based on only a few encounters, said that being in Hart's presence was not a particularly pleasant experience.

> I found him a rather icy character, remote. How can I put it? I had two distinct impressions. One was of his physical presence, and strength. The other was of abstractedness, as if he had some sense of a mystical awareness, close to egoism that said "I am a superior creature. I have been given this job of lifting people out of their ordinariness." He was not an appealing character, his aura I mean, but I knew very little of him.

But Hart's theatrical skills impressed Pinter nonetheless, even if the psychotherapeutic aspects of Hart's teaching unnerved him enough to resist getting involved. Pinter went on to say:

> Then there was the piece at the Royal Festival Hall, by Maxwell Davies [*Eight Songs for a Mad King*]. He had a remarkable presence, and what he did with his voice was an extraordinary skill and gift…. But I wouldn't touch it with a barge pole because of the power he assumed and was invested in him. It seems that he was using it to investigate…[pause] the souls of those around him. The role of therapist is a highly responsible role, and this worried me. What right had he [to make these investigations]?

When I told Pinter that Hart's work had actually been instrumental in enabling me to find a way out of my own psychologically disturbed state, he replied that he was glad to hear it, although he thought that all of us had come to Roy because of psychological difficulties.[21]

---

[21] Pinter enquired about the other members of the group, and what had happened after Hart's death, which he viewed as a tragic event. Knowing that Barry Coghlan may well have encouraged Pinter to join the Club, as he was his weekly house cleaner at that time, I told Pinter of Coghlan's death in 1983, which visibly touched him. After telling him about others, I told how the group had continued to function creatively until the mid-80s, a fact which also impressed him since Pinter was suspicious that Hart was a guru and that after his death the group would have disintegrated almost immediately.

A God Above God

The Roy Hart Speakers/Singers, as we were called then, made their public theatrical debut at the World Theatre Festival in Nancy, France, in February of 1969. This was to be the first time the work of Roy Hart's students were viewed in a specifically theatrical context, and the group was scheduled to perform four times. The Festival, which was a yearly event that took place under the direction of Jack Lang, had gained a reputation for presenting innovative theatre work by younger groups. I had been to the Festival six years previously to support a play performed by the Birmingham University Drama Society which included Evan Parker's jazz quartet. Now I was there as a performer, a shift in roles that was meaningful to me.[22]

Between sessions with Roy, I continued my day job, improved my squash, continued my weekly singing lessons, and got to know other group members. A long-lost feeling of continuity returned for me, and I moved into a flat with Alan Codd. Once again being part of "Pikes & Codd" became an important bridge to my former life. It was at this time that Richard Armstrong and Vivienne Young, with whom Alan had been a student at Newcastle, began to attend the group regularly.

There were other visitors to our bacchic rites who found Roy's style of teaching disturbing. One was the theatre reviewer of the *Sunday Telegraph*, Frank Marcus, who described the group in an article dated December 1, 1968, as "Mr. Hart's psychotherapy class of some 20 actors (patients?)." Not wishing to comment on the therapeutic dimension, he "wondered if Mr. Hart had stretched the range of theatrical experience and whether his ideas were capable of wider application." He found "the frequent references, some of them (deliberately?) banal, such as one finds in the films of Godard and on the latest LP of the Beatles an eclectic choice by any standard." Marcus referred to the individual

---

[22] It was at this Festival that I first performed the role of the Herdsman as a duo with Paul Silber. Eventually I was given the role alone. I was dimly aware that in a language of images and metaphors, the Herdsman was telling part of my own story when he recounts to Pentheus all he has witnessed on Mount Kythyron. I saw that I had tried to experience Dionysos and his divinity from a hiding place in my mind through drug use and had fallen into an abyss resulting in dismemberment and madness. Now, I imagined, I was on the road to re-membering myself, a re-birth that would lead to knowledge.

poems and songs, and it seems he had been treated to such standards as "Happy Birthday" and "The Lord's Prayer." In Roy's work he found comparisons and contrasts with the work of Peter Brook and Grotowski but felt the work most conjured the "ghost of Artaud; the prophet of unreason." Marcus concluded: "Mr. Hart has welded together a group of disparate individuals into a single body: their limbs intermingled like the tentacles of an octopus, the voices belonged to all. In an atmosphere of sectarian intensity Mr. Hart exercised the 20-headed monster of his creation. It was an enthralling but slightly menacing experience."

Roy had recently moved his studio to Belsize Park, an area a little nearer to central London frequented by writers, journalists, artists, and show business people. The studio was part of a new building, the Abraxas Club, itself built on the site of and including the Hampstead Squash Club, where group members had been playing for years. There were now four squash courts plus a second floor with a gym, sauna, and massage room, and a smaller third floor housed Roy's study and the studio. All this had been the work of Monty Crawford, a member of the group who was an accountant by profession but had become a property developer. Crawford, Louis Frenkel, another exiled South African and a private investor,[23] and Roy were the three directors of this new health and sports center. At the time, the center was to become a home for furthering Roy's vision of "an integrated mind/body relationship in the individual." The club's name Abraxas seems to have its origins in ancient Gnostic teaching and is the central divinity in C. G. Jung's *Seven Sermons to the Dead* where it is called "unreal reality:" "This is a god whom ye knew not, for mankind forgot it. We name it by its name ABRAXAS. It is more indefinite still than god and devil."[24] As the union of opposites, Roy had adopted "Abraxas" as his guiding principle and spoke of it at the Sixth International Conference for Psychodrama in Zagreb:

> I am a South African Jew. But it has been necessary for me
> to find even Adolf Hitler, a South African Negro, a South
> African white man, and besides all the good, all the evil of this
> world in myself.... Realising the relation between the aggres-

---

[23] Louis Frenkel suffered from a difficult stammer which disappeared when he played Pentheus.

[24] C. G. Jung, *VII Sermones ad Mortuos*, trans. H. G. Baynes (1925; rpt. London: Robinson & Watkins, 1967) 17. Herman Hesse also refers to "Abraxas" in *Steppenwolf.*

sor and victim is in myself I worship the god of synthesis.
That is why I have called my Abraxas Club by his name.[25]

The Club's directors generous attitude towards group members, included the absence of monetary payments to Roy for our education (apart from individual voice lessons) and an honorary membership to the Club. In return we sometimes helped with work that needed to be done there. It seemed that everybody contributed during the construction and renovation. I worked many hours on mosaics designed by Paul Silber for the showers and entrance to the club. Later some members were paid for their work. The dancers, led by Robert Harvey, began to offer movement classes to music with a keep-fit orientation. Ronald Andrews (a television repairman who had joined the group after meeting Roy while fixing his set) and Paul Silber, became gym and fitness trainers for men. Diane Palmer, a young Canadian with secretarial experience, ran reception, and several of the group worked part-time in the Club's restaurant and bar. Alan Codd became the cleaner, and later I joined him at this task. Bill Ashford, the professional squash coach in the former Club, continued to work there, although he was not a member of the group. The new venture began with relative success. Among the squash players were writer Alan Alvarez and Harold Pinter (whose flat was cleaned by Barry, one of the dancers). Several members of Monty Python's Flying Circus, including John Cleese and Michael Palin, also joined the Club.

It was into the Abraxas Club's green tiled corridors and multi-coloured mosaics, smelling vaguely of sweat and squash balls, that a group of young German student protest leaders breezed one morning, shortly after the place had opened. Among this group was Daniel Cohn-Bendit, nicknamed "Danny the Red,"[26] and Gaston Salvatore, a militant Chilean writer. Salvatore had written a poem on the necessity for revolt which had been set to music written in 1968 by a member of this group, Hans Werner Henze (now a famous composer). Roy was to interpret this work at its premier with the Philip Jones Brass Ensemble. It was entitled *Versuch Über Schweine*, or "Essay on Pigs;" *Schweine* being the name given to the student protesters by the German bourgeoisie. Henze and his companions were at Abraxas to complete preparations for the event.

---

[25] *Svobodne Slovo*, Zagreb, 21 May 1970.
[26] Daniel Cohn-Bendit is now a Green member of the European Parliament.

The composers' interest in Roy as a solo performer began when Roy sent them a tape recording of his voice. The recording, which begins with Roy exploring the three opening words of *The Bacchae*, "I am Dionysos," featured his incredible "chorded" sounds where his voice produces three separate strands at the same time. Upon hearing that tape, Henze wrote to Roy, "This tape and your letter have reached me at a moment of great changes in my music and aesthetics, and maybe it could mean something really important for the development of things in art."[27] Roy began work on the score for *Versuch Über Schweine* in his new studio towards the end of 1968, devoting several hours each day to preparing his performance.

I witnessed this performance of Roy's at The Queen Elizabeth Hall, a prestigious London concert hall, on 14 February 1969. It was only the second time since he had left RADA that he performed on stage. His poise, bodily engagement, control of his voice and the German language impressed me. He was centred and present, and while it was the Roy I thought I was beginning to know, witnessing him perform obliged me to reappraise him. The work was released by Deutsche Grammophon, although for several years it was withdrawn at Henze's request.[28]

But Roy was just getting started. A few months later, on April 22, in the same hall, Roy was the solo vocalist in the premier of a work that marked the emergence of a new form of performance, called "music theatre." Written by Peter Maxwell Davies, the work was what Davies' biographer, M. Seabrook, describes as a kind of divine madness:

> At the time many people found this work [*Eight Songs for a Mad King*] variously offensive, horrifying, incomprehensible or plain mad. Although since then it has become accepted as a work of genius, and (to Max's great satisfaction) no longer leaves people mystified or repelled (at least, not so many people), it is still a profoundly disturbing work. It is a ferocious portrayal of insanity, and on first hearing its main effect is genuinely shocking.[29]

---

[27] Letter to Roy Hart dated September 4, 1967. Roy Hart Theatre Archives, Malérargues, France.

[28] *Versuch Über Schweine*, with Hart as soloist, is now part of *The Henze Collection* [Deutsche Grammophon 449 869-2 (GC)].

[29] M. Seabrook, *The Life and Music of Peter Maxwell Davies* (London: Victor Gollancz, 1994) 108.

Dressed in a robe and hat while the five musicians of the Pierrot Players were imprisoned in giant aluminium bird cages, Roy brought George III to life in this performance. The texts of the piece were written by Randolph Stow, many of them adapted from things that George III is alleged to have actually said, written, and done. Roy portrayed the King's well-known habit of talking to birds in the Palace aviary by chirping and sounding like a bird to a flautist who replied with her instrument. Later in the performance, Roy as King snatched a violin from its player only to break it, and in the last "song," the King became extremely lucid, pronouncing on his own fate as if he were merely an informed observer. Roy as King said that he "...covered the mirrors with black currant jelly so as not to see himself pass by.... Poor fellow, he will die...howling, howowowling, how-how-hooooowling...." Roy built this last word to an awesome crescendo as he walked off stage followed by musicians in a solemn procession marching to a slow, rhythmic beating of a bass drum that slowly faded as they disappeared into the wings.

The effect of Roy's performance was nothing less than royal. Audience members sometimes addressed him after the show as if he were a king, and he received compliments and follow-up correspondence from Princess Alexandra. Author and educator George Steiner, who heard the performance on the radio, wrote Roy to say, "Last night's performance on the BBC was a stunning experience. I think it may well be a work of genius, but pivoting wholly on your gifts."[30] Maxwell Davies wrote on Roy's copy of the score, "For Roy—with infinite thanks and gratitude for a magnificent splendid job. Much love. Max."[31] The work was performed at least twelve more times in the following months at festivals in the United Kingdom, France, and Vienna, and it was televised by *Norddeutsche Rundfunk* in Hamburg, Germany. A recording and a film were planned.

But the phenomenal success of the performance bred a dispute between Roy and Davies concerning whose work it really was. Richard Armstrong, who was responsible for the costumes and bird cages on the stage set and who closely followed the work's early stages, said there were considerable exchanges between the two men as Roy explored possible interpretations of Stow's words. According to Armstrong, both

---

[30] From a letter to Roy Hart, Roy Hart Theatre Archives, Malérargues, France.
[31] Roy Hart's original score of *Eight Songs for a Mad King*. RHT Archives.

men were responsible for the success of the piece: "The work was totally collaborative."[32] Initially Roy explored the eight texts by improvising.
Later his interpretations of the eight texts stabilised, which he then recorded, and it was around this recording that Davies wrote his music.[33]

Yet Roy's disdain at being treated as merely "the vocalist" could not
be overcome, and he eventually broke off contact with Davies. Kevin
Crawford later recalled that he tried to heal the split:

> I and Alan Codd wrote a long letter on Roy's behalf that
> I actually read aloud to Davies and his agent, James Murdoch.
> The reading took a good half-hour and spoke of Roy's belief
> that his artistic gifts were based on the deep integrity of his
> moral and personal fabric. His vocal freedom had been earned
> at the price of personal self-discipline and a re-visioning of the
> boundaries between the artist and the person. These things
> were not "commodities" to be bought or bargained for. Roy
> felt that Davies could not acknowledge this and after my
> reading the schism was never bridged.[34]

Despite their efforts the reading did not work, and the relationship ended.
Later Roy expressed sadness that the collaboration had not continued
and acknowledged that it was this work that he had most enjoyed.

Improvisation as Treason

Undaunted, Roy entered into another collaboration in 1969, this time
with avant-garde German composer Karlheinz Stockhausen. After
a brief correspondence that began when Stockhausen heard the presentation recording of Roy's voice work, the composer visited Abraxas
in time to watch a rehearsal of *The Bacchae*.[35] During the rehearsal, Roy
asked us to lie on our backs and keep our legs at a forty-five degree

---

[32] Richard Armstrong, from an interview with the author.

[33] This information is not mentioned in the books I have read about Davies' work.
Although Paul Griffiths in *Peter Maxwell Davies* (London: Robson Books, 1982) does
acknowledge that the score requires "an extraordinary range of over five octaves and a
variety of weird effects stimulated by the outlandish virtuosity of Roy Hart."

[34] From a private letter dated 1998 in the author's papers.

[35] Before his visit to Abraxas, Karlheinz Stockhausen wrote to Hart: "After having
listened to your tape I wish to write to you immediately. Your technique makes possible
what a few experimental composers have been seeking for several years. BRAVO!!"
From a letter to Roy Hart dated October 19, 1968, Roy Hart Theatre Archives.

angle for as long as possible. After a short time, we found ourselves involuntarily uttering sounds that were obviously alien to Stockhausen. The experience impressed him, and Roy was later invited to perform Stockhausen's adaptation of his now famous *Spirale*. Together with several musicians, Roy performed the work one early summer evening in the flower-scented gardens of the Fondation Maeght art collection in St. Paul de Vence, France. Roy's singing seemed to be complemented by the extraordinarily beautiful setting, and some months later the two men collaborated again at the International Seminar of New Music in Darmstadt, Germany. Roy performed *Aus den Sieben Tagen* and *Abwärts* at the event, leaving critics mystified by his talents.

> He could be taken for a well-bred and brilliant sixth-former, if it weren't for the distinctive creases in his face that speak of a man in his forties. His English is of silken splendour; you could not have guessed that during the concert he had bellowed like a stag, imitated baby cries, frogs croaking and the whistle of a kettle at full steam....
>
> The public experienced him as a grandiose actor, dancer and mime, as a comedian, as the singer with the ghost like voice-ladder. He leaps like a flea, like an Orangutan, grimaces into the camera like a clown, volleys a tennis ball, trips and convulses himself in an aria of hysterical laughter. He moves on the edge of his intuition and Stockhausen's fixed composition.[36]

But, like Roy's other collaborations, things turned sour when Stockhausen took exception to Roy's improvised interpretation of his score. The composer went so far as to stage a mock trial after the performance with the audience as jury, the charge being that Roy was guilty of treason to the arts. When Roy returned to London, he did not share this experience with members of the group, but Jean-Pierre Drouet, now a leading French percussionist, witnessed the event and recounted the story to Richard Armstrong. Although it is not clear if Roy was found "guilty" by his audience, a review from the performance indicated that Roy defended his position by saying he "believed they [Stockhausen and Hart] would have found a bridge had there been a

[36] From *Darmstadter Echo*, Sept. 7, 1969.

clarifying rehearsal before the performance." Stockhausen's dramatic manoeuver was not universally appreciated, however. Drouet refused to take part in the trial and never performed with Stockhausen again.

Roy may have in fact improvised during Stockhausen's work. Although he normally respected written scores when collaborating with living composers, Roy would often use improvisation when directing performances of the group, and he demanded improvisations from us, both in rehearsals and performances. For instance in December 1969, the newly named Roy Hart Theatre gave a performance of *The Bacchae as The Frontae*, with a post-Nietzschian subtitle, "Language is Dead, Long Live the Voice." Advertisements for the play were displayed on the walls outside of London's leading avant-garde theatre, a former steam-train engine shed called "The Roundhouse." As we prepared the death of Pentheus, Roy instructed me and Kevin Crawford to commentate on the event as if we were television reporters, me from the BBC and Kevin from a commercial channel. I pretended to hold a microphone and separated myself from the chorus to address the audience as if it were news:

> Here I am on the slopes of a Greek mountain side, Cithyron, reputed to have been the home of the gods. It's been reported that a group of women, some of them from wealthy families, have been dancing, singing, and indulging in all kinds of strange and unladylike activities. As I look around me, I can see some women over there pulling down a tall pine tree. Yes, as I get closer I see they are pulling someone out of the upper branches…. I can't tell if it's a man or woman…. Now I can see women's clothes…. But, as I get closer, I see a man's face. His yells are desperate and as the women hold him high above their heads, he seems as light as a feather! Now I am really very close and what I see is horrendous….

At another time during the performance, Roy, who was directing on stage while sitting at a piano mounted on two large wooden cart wheels, jumped up and grabbed the cart's two handles, ran around the stage forcing us to break up our acting and react to this whirl of energy. The improvisation did not end there. Later, fifty large square white cards each with a letter were suddenly strewn across the stage. Like ants possessed we worked to peg them up on a horizontal string which read, "THE MOMENT OF GREATEST PERIL COINCIDES WITH THE MOMENT OF GREATEST HOPE."

Kevin Crawford, son of Monty Crawford and a recent arrival in the group at the time, remembers that improvisation was an integral part of that performance:

> [I remember] an unplanned entrance onto the stage of a member of the audience during the scenes concerning the dismemberment, death, and laying out of Pentheus. This person comes on the stage and is immediately integrated into the show without even a split-second's hesitation, as if it was predestined. He lies down on the stage alongside the inert body of Pentheus, and both are covered over with a cloth for the final scenes of mad ecstacy and horror. At the end I stand for what feels like an eternity on the stage drinking in the immensity of this experience where a stranger has shared and amplified our journey on stage. Finally I leave the stage, and my gaze crosses Roy Hart's. He must have seen something in my face for he looks at me intensely and talks about my spiritual reaction to the events of the evening and my "high" seriousness. I leave the theatre still burning with the fresh memory of this extraordinary apparition in the performance.[37]

But Roy was far from embracing the idea of "happenings," believing them to be "a momentary escape; it is creative work which interests me—which supposes relationship, time, honour, loyalty, and dedication to life."[38] Instead, the performance was grounded in the work on *The Bacchae,* although much of Euripides' original script had gradually been replaced by other elements that had emerged during the previous month's meetings and rehearsals. Improvisations were sometimes Roy's ideas, but just as often they were brought in by group members. By being able to stage creative impulses from the individual and group psyches through texts, songs, images, and dreams, "we extract[ed] from the text that which is present in us."[39] The improvised elements deepened the concentration and excitement already heightened by working before an audience of more than three hundred in a large space.

---

[37] From a letter dated 1997 in the author's archives.
[38] From *Primer Acto.*
[39] From *Primer Acto.*

Had I been asked whether I was engaged in performing theatre or participating in research in a new form of expressive therapy, I would not have felt the distinction to be relevant. I believe the melding of these two perspectives was unique to Roy at that time. This was not always easy for the audience to understand, and reviewers drew varying conclusions. One writer from the *Sunday Times* saw "Roy Hart as guru" and felt excluded from the event, perhaps because he was unable to join in "the agonised panting and obligatory orgasms" he "saw." Another reviewer from *The Daily Telegraph* also felt excluded from a "ritualised cacophony of mime and movement, though lacking the physical and political arrogance of the Living Theatre…. Roy Hart aims not to entertain. He succeeds triumphantly!" Yet another reviewer from *Time Out* who had seen *Hair* had no doubt that "*Hair* was a less exciting experience and a bit of a fraud. I did not believe what its actors preached because I could see that they didn't."[40] H. Kretzmer of the *Daily Express* enjoyed "an orgy of therapy" and had "never seen actors giving quite so much of themselves," while de Jongh, from *The Guardian*, concluded that Roy's group performance was "…an evening in which technique is superbly in evidence."

Therapist and publisher Derek Gale, then a student, first encountered the Roy Hart Theatre at this event and saw how the audience response was mixed: "[It was] a performance which seemed to span theatre and dance in all its forms, from the most ancient and primitive to the most modern. Probably only in the 60s could such a thing have been performed and accepted, although it must be said that some did not, as there were shouts of protest from the audience."[41] There had also been a shout from the audience in the same theatre a few weeks previously when the "Living Theatre," a group often compared to Roy Hart Theatre, performed *Paradise Now*. That shout came from Roy Hart himself: "Dangerous nonsense!"

On the Road

By 1970 the long-awaited dream of finding composers who could write for "the voice of the future" had not only been realised, it was

---

[40] J. Abulafia, *Time Out*, Dec. 6, 1969.

[41] From a letter dated 1997 in the author's papers.

consigned to history—at least by Roy. Although he seemed to be shifting his focus away from the group, Roy was still working on his central thesis: that voice was an expression of the soul. In an interview in Nancy, France, with a journalist from *L'est Républicain*, Roy said that "the voice is the muscle of the soul," a phrase he used to describe the essence of his approach and one which has since been often quoted. Roy added that "it [voice] is the best way to express the contradictory demons which dwell in man," and that he wanted to "go beyond 'beauty' to discover all man's vocal possibilities." Referring to the three musical compositions recently written for his voice, whose themes he described as revolt, madness, and electronics, he observed, "These are three principal characteristics of our civilisation and the voice is perfectly capable of expressing these concepts." For his part, the journalist observed that, "Mr. Hart is not an impassioned character in that the flow of his speech is regular, his words are considered and his expressions chosen."

Now Roy no longer gave individual singing lessons to members of the group, but he had begun to give lessons outside of Roy Hart Theatre. Jack Lang was a lawyer, Director of the Department for Theatre Research at the University of Nancy, subsequently Minister for Culture and Minister for Education in France. As organizer of the Nancy World Theatre Festival in 1969, Lang had found its most impressive performance was *The Bacchae*, and he had invited Roy back to give a ten day seminar to his students. Roy accepted, and at the end of April, 1970 (exactly one year after *The Bacchae* had first been performed), Roy gave his first "workshop," and Jack Lang received his first "singing lesson."

Meanwhile, the group was engaged in intensive evening rehearsals with the group in order to prepare for an upcoming performance at the Festival of San Sebastian in northwestern Spain. The performance, which was eventually called *A Song of Everest,* consisted of two parts. The first was constructed around a tape recording of Roy performing the *Eight Songs for a Mad King*, and the second part was a group collage based on an evolving *Bacchae* (called *The Bacchae as The Frontae*). As an opening, we improvised movement to the tape recording which then led to a small group, including myself, miming the instrumentalists while Roy would improvise live over his own recorded voice. Following the recent break with Maxwell Davies, Roy wanted to demonstrate his asser- tion that while musicians are dispensable, the voice is not as it is the true source of music. For the second part, Richard Armstrong and Vivienne Young had made costumes designed to display something of each individual's archetypal character. Roy was dressed as a cowboy, Anna Allen was in a judo outfit, Angela Bland was dressed as a nun, and I was given the costume of a convict.

The group now had over thirty members, and many of the new-comers were of my own generation of "soul seekers." There were three students from a photography school in West London—David Goldsworthy, Kenneth Clarke, and James Ryan—as well as three brothers by the name of Rivers-Moore. My sister, Margaret, a child-hood friend of Vivienne Young, had now finished her studies and had brought her painter boyfriend. About twenty of the members were going to San Sebastian to be in the Festival production, and the rest were to stay behind to run the Abraxas Club.

A few days prior to the Festival, Paul Silber, his wife Nadine, and I were invited to Nancy by train in order to join Roy. Once we met Roy in Nancy, our plan was to travel with him to San Sebastian by car, a trip that would take us across France. It was an exciting prospect. Roy's invitation to join him on the journey was a new departure, as he had always travelled with Dorothy, Lizzie, and her partner, Louis Frenkel, when-ever he went abroad. At Hart's suggestion some years earlier, Louis had purchased a chalet in Anzère, a ski resort in the Swiss Alps, which he named "Chalet Awe" in honour of Alfred Wolfsohn. This small group would go to the chalet several times a year to enjoy skiing, walking, and dining out. These were not things I had experienced in my hitchhiking travels across Europe, and I was eagerly awaiting the experience of getting to know Roy in this context, completely reversing my earlier rejection of such bourgeois behaviour.

We may have been invited so that we could deliver a short film directed by a young man who called himself Saturn Kiev. I had introduced Kiev to Roy a few months earlier after meeting him on one of my occasional outings into the alternative London scene. The film, which used a small number of the group in the depiction of an imagined religious ritual, was filmed on one of the squash courts, giving the soundtrack an odd echoing quality. Hart's idea was to include the film in the live demonstration he was to give at the end of his seminar. However, the film was sent finally by mail, and we arrived in Nancy after the event had ended.

Once we arrived, we set out from Nancy in Louis Frenkel's large Volvo, a car which I sometimes washed and cleaned to supplement my modest income. The driving was shared between the three men—Paul, Roy, and myself. It was the first time I had driven on the right hand side of the road, but Roy seemed to have complete confidence in my driving ability and fell asleep next to me after our first lunch. Roy paid for this meal by producing an impressive-sized wad of notes that held about two thousand French francs, the result of his work at the Nancy seminar. In fact Roy paid for all our expenses during this journey, a move that revealed to me both his generosity and his disdain for money.

On route we learned that, once more, Roy and his collaborator had suffered a break in their working relationship. This time, Roy and Lang had been involved in a discussion about Israel and Palestine in which Roy had sided with the Jews and Lang had taken up the defense of the Arabs. For Roy, Israel stood for the realisation of a dream held for thousands of years, a dream expressed in the well-known phrase, "Next year in Jerusalem." He saw the creation of Israel as symbolic of the only possible way forward for humanity through the creation of such "synthetic families." The argument escalated, and no Abraxian synthesis being found, the relationship was severed.

The first evening of our journey, we arrived in a village on the Atlantic coast, south of Bordeaux, in a flat area known as *les Landes* which is covered in small pines and sand dunes. We found rooms for the night, but finding no restaurant, we entered a bar, something Roy would rarely do. Having no luck there, a dinner consisting of bread and cheese with a little red wine was served in Roy's bedroom. During this unusual repast, Roy sat on the bed. After years of gruelling rehearsals and lessons, it was the first informal contact I had with Roy, and I jokingly said at the time that it would be one that I would recall in his biography.

The next day we drove south past surfers on the giant waves of Biarritz to meet up with the group at San Sebastian in the afternoon. It did not take long after we arrived to learn that our first performance in Spain might not go smoothly. At the time Spain was still under the dictatorship of General Franco, although pressure for his withdrawal had been building for some time. Under Franco's orders certain radical theatre groups had been excluded from the festival, and as a an act of solidarity, other groups were being asked by local Basque Nationalists not to perform. However, Roy believed that the idea of "performance" transcended political maneuvers, that it partook of the eternal and not of the temporal, and rejected their proposal thinking that might put an end to the problem. But the following day when we arrived at the theatre prior to the performance, we found the entire building surrounded by members of the *Guardia Civil.* Once inside, we were told of a plan to prevent our performance from taking place. Nevertheless, Roy directed us to go ahead, and the curtain went up on a full house at the appointed hour.

The recording of *Eight Songs for a Mad King* began to play, and we began our performance by improvising on stage. A few seconds later there were loud calls from several young men in the auditorium, and a group of about twenty protesters surged forward, leaped across the orchestra pit, and jumped on stage. "Freeze!" hissed Roy, and the group came to a theatrical standstill as the protesters moved among us. It was a tense moment. Roy was waiting to see if any kind of dialogue might be possible on stage, which he certainly would have viewed as theatre. However, as the protesters' aggression, and no doubt frustration, began to mount, Roy gave us the signal to abandon the stage, leaving the protesters up there to put on their own show.[42]

The experience in Spain seemed to put the theatre into a temporary tailspin, and *A Song of Everest* was performed just once, a month later in Rennes, France, although I was not there—probably because of my "negative aura" at the time. According to Derek Rosen "the piece was a disaster because *The Bacchae* was over, and we didn't really have another one ready. There was no structure. It was all improvised. We didn't know what the hell we were doing."[43] This lack of structure was evident to the audience. A reviewer for *Ouest-France* found the first part to be "extraordinary, being able even to provoke physical reactions in the public." But he found the second part inferior and regretted that "there had been no psychological preparation of the public, in one form or another."[44]

---

[42] After we left the stage, we quietly changed, left, and filed past the policemen to meet in a restaurant. But although this first performance in Spain had been aborted, Hart and the Roy Hart Theatre were destined to develop a close relationship with that country over the next eighteen months.

[43] From an interview with the author.

[44] *Ouest-France*, June 4, 1970.

Derek Rosen remembers how difficult the performance was, and how one woman in the group, Angela Bland, managed to save the event:[45]

> The sparse audience of students in Rennes had reacted quite vocally themselves when the second part began, with catcalls, boos and shrieks. As we didn't know what we were doing anyway, it was very difficult and we were just terrified! Angela, however, went out into the audience, looked at them, took their hands and sang to them, and managed to calm them down. Roy was very proud of her and called us a lot of cowards. [Laughter] She was very open, a kind of flower-power person and just charmed them.

Angela's antics continued the next day, much to the amusement of Roy. Rosen continued:

> Next day we all went to the beach and then had a late lunch in a fantastic fish restaurant where we got hysterically drunk, including Roy; we were just laughing with relief that the damn thing was over! [Laughter] Angela was outrageous, and Roy loved that. She didn't give a damn for protocol or anything like that. We were each eating a long, smoked fish, and she took hers on her fork and wiped the whole thing round Roy's face. We were absolutely aghast, but he was laughing, so it was okay! In fact he played up to her and prolonged it; it was very sensual actually. Eventually the whole fish went into his mouth in one go.

A few months later, not having been able to seduce Roy into bed and finding the whole setup "too churchy," Angela left the group.

Back to Spain

Using my experience running the University Campaign for Nuclear Disarmament, I helped with efforts to publicise the work of the Roy Hart Theatre from a small office in the Abraxas Club. Despite the

---

[45] I had known Angela Bland prior to meeting Hart, as she was one of John McWilliam's girlfriends. At the worst point in my breakdown, at the end of my stay in the jazz musicians' house in Earl's Court, John had told Angela to spend a night with me. He knew that I had sexual "problems," and he thought that a night with Angela might just sort me out. I disappointed them, but in my defence I should say that I did not actually find her desirable. I later told John to come to the Roundhouse performance, which he found completely mad, and I have never seen him since. But Angela, who accompanied him there, found it otherwise and soon after began to come to the studio.

fiasco that took place the last time the group was in Spain, a letter came inviting the Roy Hart Theatre to perform at the International Festival in Madrid in October of 1971. Roy accepted the invitation, thus re-establishing his connection to the Spanish theatre world.

The show we were to present at the Festival had evolved from the one the group prepared for San Sebastian. The first part, called *A Song of the Mind*, opened with a solo improvisation by Roy, and via movement from the group, led into the second part called *Birth Day*. Roy was not present on stage, and maybe this was the meaning of the title as this was the first time we were on stage without our director. Also the new performance depended on more nonverbal material, a change that left some reviewers breathless. José Monleon, a well-known theatre writer for *Informaciones* wrote:

> The actor expresses himself in screams and calls, in this way externalising his intimate personality, and thus creates a unity with the other actors. It is not a matter of singing, but of sending the voice from the deepest part of the body, with free but controlled delivery. From this personal and collective control, the drama...a total theatre is achieved. Roy Hart Theatre represents one of the most important experiments in communication in the restless world of the theatre today."[46]

Although one might assume the performance was difficult to follow and an uncomfortable experience for the audience, Monleon said that the audience was not lost and the performance "in its power of communication...cannot be more profound."

Monleon was the first reviewer to befriend the group. During the Festival, he took a few of us on a tour of his favourite *tapas* bars in the Plaza Major, the old part of town. Monleon also arranged a two-week visit by Roy to teach at the Higher School of Dramatic Art in March of 1971. The seminar which took place was a major event in the Spanish theatre world, and two hundred professionals, including many leading performers, attended the classes.[47] Yet it was amazing that the seminar took place at all given the political climate:

---

[46] *Informaciones*, 16 October 1967.

[47] During this time, *Primer Acto*, the monthly theatre journal, published the most in-depth interviews ever made with Roy Hart. They provide insight into how he presented his ideas to outsiders, how he taught them voice, and how they received them and him.

[The seminar] would have been inconceivable in Madrid only a few years ago...the students would have been considerably more hesitant about participating inasmuch as Roy would not align himself with either of the sacred political creeds, right or left. It is also certain that very few "established" professionals would have had the humility and integrity that is apparent amongst those who now attend every morning. Something is happening....[48]

Roy was aware of the political tension and tried to keep attention focused on theatre and the human experience. Roy said:

I came to Madrid with a strange trepidation due to previous experiences at psychotherapeutic and musical congresses, at performances and other teaching engagements in various European cities. The hunger of the individual students with whom I have come into contact here has been a most emotional experience. There is a surprising necessity to fill an emptiness, something that in general I did not meet in any other place in Europe. I here came into contact with human beings who wanted something that I seemed able to give them. The form that this took differed, as all of us in reality are unique, different and not repeatable, although the initial work I offer seeks to reveal the fundamentals of the common humanity that we all possess, independent of geographical origin or religion.

Some did not appreciate Roy's efforts to keep politics out of his seminar, and he was criticised for not acknowledging that Franco's long-standing military dictatorship was coming under ever-increasing pressure to step down. Roy was condemned by some for lacking awareness of the situation and for having "an evasive attitude that has contributed to the creation of a mystical climate." The word "mystical," like "disembodied," was a form of criticism used by Roy himself, and now it was being thrown back at him. In an interview published in March, 1971, in *Primer Acto*, Roy attempted to reply to the accusations:

Roy Hart: There are many people who are willing to struggle with a rifle and very few who are willing to take the small path. The fundamental choice is that it be an authentic struggle. One has to know oneself, to know one's real

[48] From *Primer Acto*, March 1971.

motives. If you know them, if you have a clear idea of why, I congratulate you.

  Interviewer: Yes, but the fact is that no-one ever knows himself, and meanwhile, what is there to do—stand with your arms crossed?

  Roy Hart: No! You try and make your motives authentic. During the first few years I was in England, after leaving South Africa, I felt enormous impulses to return and fight against the repressive government that came to power. Upon reflection however, I realised that my struggle was another. At first I doubted my decision; today I am happy and affirm it.

This was not the first time Roy faced political questions. The theme of revolution had come up two years earlier in *Versuch Über Schweine*, and Henze, the work's author, questioned Roy about his political motives.

[T]he first thing Henze said when we met in Amsterdam was to ask me if I knew of Chê Guevara. I assumed he wanted to know what kind of revolutionary I was, from his point of view. I answered that I sympathised with the revolution in that it is something evident in man; if a man is in organic harmony with himself, he will not have to fear the exteriorisation of his being, but if he is split by a rebellion between his body and himself then all attempts at external manifestations would be explosive and terrible. This seemed reasonable enough to him.[49]

Roy even blamed the two men's eventual split on what Roy felt were Henze's psychologically näive ideas about revolution:

He wrote a work for my voice on the theme of revolution. He heard my sounds and immediately wanted to use them for the externalisation of his own need for revolution. Shortly after the work had been recorded by Deutsche Grammophon I pointed out certain psychological facts to him, as a friend, and there has since been a rift in our relationship; to me this is quite an expected pattern.[50]

---

[49] From *Primer Acto*.

[50] *Ibid*. Roy Hart's voice can be heard in Henze's work, *Versuch Über Schweine*, issued on CD, " The Henze Collection," by Deutsche Grammophon 449 869-2 (GC).

In the program note to "Birth Day," Roy seems to address Henze's ideas on revolution directly:

> RHT [Roy Hart Theatre] are living a DAILY REVOLU-TION: those who testify to be for "THE" Revolution and fail to show it in their everyday lives, to me, literally STINK! because they are evading the central issue—how to find your own unique VOTE, embodied in a unique voice, found in a singular BODY, touched by a loving sensibility.

Perhaps José Monleon explained Roy's position on revolution most succinctly: "What good is it fighting against dictatorship if one is a small dictator in one's private life? Doesn't the rationalising ego, in its fight with the unconscious, cover up by adopting ideological arguments against the very existence of an individual reality?"

Of course Roy was not unaware of or insensitive to the struggle of the younger generation in Spain at that time. A year later, after several more seminars had been given in Madrid and Barcelona, Roy wrote that the revolutionary spirit of Spain's youth was similar to that of the group:

> The surging revolutionary spirit of the young Spain of today senses the profound meaning of the revolution we have been working on for twenty five years, in our own bodies.
>
> Of course, the politically ambitious, the dedicated revolutionary, resents the impact that our work has made, just as Henze resented my comments, but I know that I am as dedicated a revolutionary as any of them. Although I am Jewish and honour this fact, I am not in Israel helping their admirable though sadly anachronistic fight for survival. Nor would I join Henze in his allegiance to the student revolution, nor have I joined the Spaniards, despite my compassion for their cause. I know that my role is to teach people to be aware of the political explosives within themselves before they can be of any use to the cause of human progress.[51]

---

[51] *The Objective Voice*, by Roy Hart, an unpublished paper which Roy presented at the 7th International Congress of Psychodrama in Tokyo, Japan, in 1972. RHT archives.

Barry Coghlan in front of the door of the house on the Greek Aegean
island of Paxos, where many of the group spent holidays, summer 1973.

CHAPTER FIVE
"Re-education of the Personality"

At the core of Roy's teaching was his belief in the individual and his or her voice, and at the nucleus of every human being, the artist. It is these beliefs which differentiate him from the "guru" at the centre of a sect that some saw in him. But Roy's role as a teacher of life did become paramount. Roy's seminal experience with Wolfsohn, when he realised that he could have killed him, had larger implications for the artist—and perhaps political being—which can be seen in most of us. For Roy, it was through voice that one could deal with the complexities of the human experience. Ian Magilton explained how Roy's ideas translated to the everyday world:

> [D]on't pretend to be a murderer, find the murderer you are—
> and if you let him live, *sing* him (and her) he won't accidentally
> kill someone on your behalf. *There* was the inextricable link
> between art and therapy, between the artist and the man,
> without which theatre could be no-more than play acting, and
> life could be no-more than obedience to chemical, biological,
> psychological, and social conditions. This realisation implied
> that integrity for the artist must be more than a vague inten-
> tion of being 'true to oneself'; it requires that this "self" be
> discovered and honoured in all its universal dimensions.[1]

Taking the threads already identified by Wolfsohn and gathering others from many seemingly disparate fields of human enquiry, Roy wove a philosophy of life and art which he insisted could not be understood by the intellect alone but had to be lived on a daily basis. It is here that

[1] From *Voice*, a booklet edited by Ivan Midderigh of the Roy Hart Theatre, which contains texts on Wolfsohn, Hart, and Roy Hart Theatre.

Roy's "biological re-education of the personality through the voice" begins
to include not only the expression of the body but also delves into the
substrata of the unconscious bringing what is hidden there to light:

> I had to gain in my body the knowledge of my comprehensive
> humanity…. The average European singer is simply not
> embodied enough to produce the intensity of the range which
> I have demonstrated. My life's work has been to give bodily
> expression to the totality of myself. This means bringing an
> enormous unconscious territory into consciousness.[2]

Only a new artistic form, one which fused theatrical and musical
vocal expression with self-expression, could contain Roy's ideas. Although
Jenny Johnson's version of Schubert's *Erlkönig* was a step along the way
to this new form, the *Eight Songs for a Mad King* was its foundation stone.
Once the new form took shape, there seemed to be no stopping it.
"The RHT [Roy Hart Theatre] blew into the theatre with such a presence,
such a protesting violence, in the cries and songs, the gestures, the
attitudes, the movements, that their performance could only be described
as total art, never seen or heard before."[3]

But Roy broke the boundaries of the studio and began to educate
people outside the group who had no previous knowledge of his
approach and philosophy. For example, Monleon understood the links
between the seemingly separate realities of power and politics, society
and the individual psyche, theatre and working on the voice, and applied
them to the unsteady theatre world of Spain in the 70s. For Monleon,
Roy's real political strength was in his ability to reach an audience in a new
way. "Any actor can recite profound statements from a text where his
role is like that of a tape-recorder. If, however, the actor must embody
those words in some way, he must become an active element in the
communication with the spectator and his organism must galvanise itself
into action."After watching Roy teach conventionally trained actors,
Monleon concluded that the usual form of theatre was "an atrociously
crude one" where the actors have their "faces initially closed and bodies
and voices oscillating between constriction and ecstasy undergo a liberat-
ing aggression." Monleon, it seems, saw that Roy's attempts to reach

---

[2] *The Objective Voice.*
[3] From a regional newspaper review of the untitled RHT performance given in
Angers, France, during the Festival "Music and Vocal Art of our Time," 19-24 Jan. 1971.

beyond a limited European voice created, in the end, not a wild, unrestrained performer but an extremely sophisticated one:

> The taming of one's sounds must constitute a fundamental part of the taming of oneself. Because such a discovery will inevitably go beyond conventional ideas of vocal expression Roy Hart told students at the start. "If anyone is afraid of losing his voice, or of becoming hoarse you should not take part in my lessons as you certainly run the risk of doing just that."
>
> ... When Hart works with an individual the others are silent and attentive. From the piano he studies the student, speaks to him, directs him, avoids any suggestion of hypnosis, corrects him from time to time and ends each lesson with some real dramatic improvisations. Roy is asked one or two questions but what is most important are the questions that each pupil asks himself while witnessing the lesson of a friend.[4]

Within a year after his work in Spain, Roy began to earn a reputation outside of the theatre world. Guy Lafargue, a young French social psychologist and "therapist of expression" in search of new dimensions to expressive therapy received a lesson from Roy while he was in Bordeaux. Lafargue had never seen Roy's work when he came for the lesson and the experience was both harrowing and meaningful. Lafargue's account of the lesson illustrates the nature of the dialogue that Roy's "catalytic friendship" could stimulate.

> Disconcerting workshop, violent experience. Roy Hart gives individual lessons at the piano. Mixture of fascination and fascism...resistance and possession. He/it takes you by the throat and the stomach...regression? aggression...what's the boundary between psychotherapy and artistic recreation?.... Acceptance of one's own weakness, of one's heaviness. Torsions, contortions, orgasm, distress, giving birth,...exploration of sado-masochism...explosion, movement, paralysis.
>
> Anyway, Roy Hart's way of relating provokes a process of bodily analysis: analysis of the vocal phenomenon in its

---

[4] *Informaciones*, March 1971.

articulation with its emotional and sexual roots…. Brutal and
tender atmosphere: Roy Hart; Mother-Father [5]

Roy translated his theories into the language of psychology, and
even psychiatry, in his efforts to explain how his teaching techniques
worked. He wrote of the sounds and energies he worked with as:

> … a very formidable, disciplined training. They attack with the
> utmost effort of body and will the different centres of energy;
> a form of shock treatment for the cells. Certain sounds stimu-
> late the cortex, others vibrate the genitals, almost all are
> controlled by the diaphragm and the mind, while the most
> rewarding sounds involve a fine, tight-rope walking commu-
> nication between head, guts, diaphragm, finger-tips and toes….
> To put it briefly, I have often referred to my art as "Conscious
> Schizophrenia" a conscious bringing together of the many
> parts into which Western man usually likes to divide and
> subdivide himself." [6]

While Roy was probably using the word "schizophrenia" here in the
informal sense of "behaviour that seems to be motivated by contradictory or conflicting principles," [7] he did use the word in its more clinical
sense to describe a psychotic disorder as "cancer of the soul." [8] In my
experience with Roy, working with the voice was indeed a way to heal
my psychological split.

For Roy, the psychological elements of his work did not exclude
religious dimensions, such as "energy" and "spirit." Early on in his work
Roy said that "there is a voice which is pure energy," meaning that it has
a divine, perhaps even unhuman, element. This "pure energy" was also
viewed and worked with as physical, bodily energy. The work of
remembering one's dismembered body by recalling and reconnecting to

---

[5] *Cahiers du Groupe de Recherche en Expression Corporelle de Toulouse.* No. 8-9 1973. My
translation.

[6] *The Objective Voice.*

[7] *The Collins Concise Dictionary of the English Language*, 2nd Edition.

[8] The centre of the diaphragm is called the "phrenic centre," and it is here that the
impulse for involuntary vocal activity—such as laughing, crying, yawning, coughing—
has its source. A conscious partnership with the diaphragm is essential for breathing and
voice that are fulfilling. That partnership is absent in both senses of "schizophrenia,"
the person is cut from their phrenic centre. It has been commented that schizophrenics
often have high, hard, and dry voices.

the life force was the essential healing action in Roy's work. Using and controlling the whole spectrum of one's voice was its artistic expression. It was, above all, in the singing lesson that this artistic and religious development took place. After countless repetitions in infinitely variable forms, the work on the voice leads to "a biological change, and eventually, to becoming 'normal' human beings—in other words, a reflection of God."[9] Regardless of his beliefs, however, Roy mostly avoided such terms and warned that "the word 'Spirit' like so many other words, gets used frequently, and in such banal circumstances, that the terrible impact of what it implies is lost."

Roy did seem to have an ability to mirror the state of one's soul, as if he were a conscious parent. He called it "carefulness," saying, "if a person, whether he be black, yellow, or green, comes into my orbit I behave in front of him with extra 'carefulness,' that is to say, I act in front of this person with the highest artistic integrity, with all my sensibility. That is what an actor is supposed to do."[10] Paul Silber recalls that Roy's "careful" attitude:

> ...applied to casual meetings in corridors or anywhere. With his remarkable capacity to see, aided by an ear every bit as extraordinary as his voice, Roy saw and responded to you as you were on that day.... This was marvellous to experience and it could happen on a daily basis! What it did was afford you the opportunity to resonate yourself within yourself, as you were on that day. What's more, by meeting you in this way, Roy prevented you from unconsciously falling into the trap which compels you to conform to some previous image of yourself. In essence he offered you an opening for growth. And your psyche took the opening and you did grow, often in spite of yourself. You grew into yourself through his capacity to listen to you and recognise what he was hearing.[11]

In Roy's world you could be judged according to your "aura." For Roy "aura" was a word which referred to the elements in and surrounding a person constellated in a particular moment and included dream images, a look on the face, tones of voice, gesture, and behaviour.

[9] From a programme note for *AND*, 1972.
[10] From *Primer Acto*.
[11] Paul Silber, from an interview with the author.

A member of the group could be loved or hated, encouraged or discouraged, affirmed or denied based on what his or her "aura" was at the time. No action was psychologically safe. For example punctuality was deemed essential in all contexts concerning the work, and any lateness on the part of a group member, even if by just a few seconds, could be investigated to discover what that member's unconscious motivations might have been. A harsh word at breakfast or a forgotten appointment would not go unnoticed. We were observed day and night and were asked to observe ourselves and others too. What was seen, heard, and felt provided much of the material for the thrice weekly meetings of the group, and its examination formed part of the re-education process. One particularly dreaded "negative constellation," which might take over one's psyche, was referred to as "The Queen of the Night," the vengeance seeking figure in Mozart's *The Magic Flute*, referred to more colloquially within the group as "a bitch." Freeing oneself from her power was an on going effort for many of us.

Being psychologically exposed often resulted in extreme emotions. If things were going in the right direction, one could experience an elation, almost a feeling of redemption, of being amongst the chosen few. However, if things were going in the wrong direction, feelings of dejection and rejection could be painful. When a member of the group was rejected, he or she was put into the outer orbits of the solar system, to bide awhile with Saturn, Uranus, or Pluto until those darker forms of energy had gone. Roy expected us to work on ourselves, to fight the invasion of these darker energies.

Although it was understood that these energies invaded everyone at some point, in my first few years it seemed that I was invaded more than most. It was difficult. Part of my re-education was learning to recognise, and eventually to trust in and to love Roy's capacity to play Lafargue's "Mother-Father" objectively, and to learn how to put myself and my motives into question. Members of the group were not loved automatically. Instead, one was shown love for the effort made towards changing, towards awakening to the call of one's *daimon*, something it seemed Roy could readily discern.

I slowly became aware that there were others in the group who also experienced "dark nights of the soul," and Roy maintained the group's unity through his awareness of individual psychic struggles, even as he gradually increased the emphasis on becoming a performing theatre company. Roy insisted that therapy came through the group. He wrote:

> Because there is a strong communal objective, and that is a noble one, the context in which we live has proved to be therapeutic. This context works as preventive therapy for people in a high intelligence bracket, who need to learn how to keep open the bridge between intellect and feeling, people of energy who need worthy channels for that energy (and there are many such people languishing in hospitals for lack of such a context). It is also beneficial for those who are not particularly gifted, nor particularly energetic, but who have patience, humility, courage and above all a desire to grow.[12]

Nevertheless, Roy recognised that what was required was not possible for everyone; he referred to the necessity of "an X factor." This view contributed to the criticism that sometimes labeled him an élitist.

> It is not suitable for those whose body chemistry has been so far influenced by traumatic experiences or a stubborn death-wish so that the will for action has been warped beyond repair. Yet who, even the most experienced of doctors, can say for certain *when* the will has been warped beyond repair? I have had some happy surprises and some sad disappointments, but my system is such that each psyche is left free to find its own level. The door is open for those who want to come to work with me. Those for whom this work would be dangerous either have the instinct to get out of the door quickly of their own accord, or occasionally have had to be guided away from it in a subtle way that leaves them without remorse or a sense of loss. It takes respect for change and stability and a great generosity of spirit to be able to stay in my theatre community for any length of time, but I have watched people who were trapped in a one-octave way of living growing towards the eight-octave life in disciplined freedom.
>
> I think of two girls who were so severely schizophrenic in their behaviour that a psychiatrist colleague of mine, insisted they were in need of hospitalisation at a certain point, but our context was strong enough to "hold" them without the need for their hospitalisation. They are both now creative assets in

---

[12] *The Objective Voice.*

RHT [Roy Hart Theatre] productions and in their daily jobs.
Three men, long established in practising homosexuality, have
been able to discover the possibilities of sustained and loving
heterosexual relationship, with interesting reflections in voice
and other behaviour.[13]

When asked how one might join Roy Hart Theatre, he stressed that
a sense of community was paramount. Unlike other theatre groups, he
did not require either vocal or theatrical skills of new members.

The members of RHT [Roy Hart Theatre] live in communal
form, in various shared flats or houses. To become a member
one first talks with me: then he works with the group for a
certain amount of time to see if his personality adapts to living
with other people or not. The capacity for living together is the
only criterion for selection. We do not look for youth or beauty
in people but rather for people who want to work and who are
compatible with the others. There is no problem when someone wants to leave the group.[14]

However, Roy and his philosophy were not free of contradictions.
When he spoke of Roy Hart Theatre as a therapy group, he was its
ultimate leader ("my system"), to the extent that he could ignore the
warnings of a psychiatrist, and when he spoke of the group as theatre,
he called it "my theatre." On the other hand, he asserted that he did not
set out to form a group. At such times he said he was the leader of the
group because of his commitment to his own voice, "which gave him a
conscience." He believed that, "the members of the group have united
in the pursuit of an idea that is much greater than me, my self or the self
in each one of us. They stay with me because they want to continue this
idea." And he was embarrassed about his name in the title of the group,
saying that "Theatre" was the important word in it. Nevertheless, he
never dropped it. There was a tension between these two poles, a
contradiction which Roy found hard to contain in the coming years.

Roy was aware of the difficulty of presenting his work in written
form and declined to write a book, stating that "I am the book," or
"You, the RHT, are the book." According to Paul Silber:

---

[13] *The Objective Voice.*

[14] From *Primer Acto.*

... Roy was aware of the transitory or relative nature of truth. That is why he resisted factual statements, especially when writing. He knew that he could make a statement to a group of people one day and on the next tell them the opposite and yet remain true. This of course made life extremely challenging. One day you would believe you had understood one thing only to find on the next that you had not understood it at all! Like most people, we preferred to believe that a statement made was a statement made, and that it could not be changed on a daily basis. But slowly we came to understand that there was a truth, which in order to remain true, had to vary according to circumstance.[15]

Although Roy was wary of fixing the truth by committing it to paper, there were occasions when members of the group did receive written messages pertinent to the member's "soul state." It would often be Diane Clark on the reception desk who would smilingly hand them to the unsuspecting recipient. The written messages often came when Roy and his small group of travelling companions were away from London. The notes were often on the back of postcards, but they could also extend into long, handwritten letters. His writing style was dense and telegramatic, characterised by word plays and puns. Often the writing on the postcards he sent would be associated with the picture on the other side. On one occasion Roy sent a book of reproduced drawings called *People*, by Eva Frankfurter, addressed to "My Beloved Theatre." Each drawing was annotated by him, naming individuals, or offering insights into how he viewed people, himself, the world, and his work. One illustration is of a chef looking at a large menu being read by another man. Roy's comment reads: "How does it feel to have the head cooked by the Stomach out of its rawness into its ROARNESS." One picture bore the inscription, "Dennis my beloved peasant"—a message to be repeated another time on the back of a postcard of a sunset on the Matterhorn.

My Dear Peasant Dennis,
Yes...My...Dear...Peasant...Dennis. You have been in my thoughts since I named your TIME Dear Dennis...IS COMING...I am happy to sense, when you will thou with me as often as THY wish.

---

[15] From "Who was Roy Hart?" a privately printed essay by Paul Silber.

I read this message with mixed feelings. On the one hand I was elated about my time "coming" but depressed at the insistence on my earthy nature.

It was a later card that carried the invitation to consider changing my name:

> [H]ow does the name NOACH feel to you. This (by the way)
> was my father's NAME.
>> your sun
>> Roy

Although I did not initially care much for the guttural "ch" at the end of the name, after a week or so of reflection, the name seemed to point to something beyond my peasanthood, and on Roy's return, I announced the change. It was immediately respected by all in the group.

The practice of name changing, especially among the males in the group, developed during this period. Whether Roy had chosen the new name or not, the name would always need to be agreed upon by him. Some chose their own names while Ann Cook and Pascale Dussau received names through dreams. Ann changed her name to Orlanda and Pascale legally changed her family name (to the distress of her French parents) to Ben. Derek Rosen became Rossignol, Ron became Hans. Like myself, other men were offered the names of Biblical figures, so Kenneth became Joseph and James became Saule. In general, a name change was an acknowledgment of change on a psychic level, and often it proved to be a help at a certain phase of separating from historical patterns of thought, judgement, and behaviour.

However, the biological births of members of the group were not forgotten. Birthdays were always honoured in some way, regardless of present "aura," and the celebration included singing "Happy Birthday." As the group increased in size, the song was extended rhythmically, harmonically, and dynamically, stretching into wonderfully exotic and unique versions. Parents were also not to be forgotten, although Roy had found that "the work caused father to turn against son, daughter against mother and friend against friend." Work on the family relationship was encouraged, and "there was sometimes a reunion with the individual's natural family or earlier friends on a new and higher level." This was true in my case, since the turns I had made away from a career had given my parents worry. Roy encouraged me to renew my relationship with them, and more than once he lent me his car to go and visit them.[16]

The Alchemist

A round 1972 group meetings were separated from rehearsals and re-named "Rivers." The name originated with the idea that projections, auras, violence, parents, the *Queen of the Night*, name changes, and dreams were the silt—our *prima materia*—which Roy, as master alchemist, would pan in search of the gold that could liberate the voice. The usual venue for Rivers was Roy's studio on the second floor of the Abraxas Club. Members often mentally prepared themselves before-hand in the long, quiet queue that developed on the stairs leading up to the studio. By now the group was forty strong, and new members included people from Spain and South America as well as Heide Hildebrand, the owner of a Viennese art gallery.[17]

The studio door always opened punctually, and we filed in, though more than once we were immediately commanded to go out and "try again." Roy's eye and ear for what he referred to as "the mysterious organisation of minute matter" was acute, and for him the performance began in the wings. One entered with a certain reverence into the white rectangular room with three, sound-insulated, double windows. The room

---

[16] A few years earlier my mother had been diagnosed as a schizophrenic and hospitalised following an attempt to leave my father and train as a nurse. During another crisis, following an affair, she came to me and my sister, Margaret, for help. During the stressful month she spent in Margaret, Richard, and Vivienne's flat, she received considerable support from us and others in the group. She attended some movement classes, and at one point seemed on the edge of a breakthrough. Alice even re-named herself Sally, a play on her name. However, in Hart's terminology, her body chemistry won the battle, and she went off to trouble her friend Mary, Vivienne's mother, eventually to be hospitalised some days later.

I re-established regular letter contact and occasional visits with my father, on one occasion spending the day at a Hampshire County cricket match with him. I learned that through renewing contact with them, and being "care-ful" about how I behaved, I could recognise aspects of my mother and father in myself. This was far from pleasant but proved to be an essential first step in gaining distance from my parental inheritance, and in a way, of giving birth to my new identity, as I was now named Noach.

[17] Heide Hildebrand had been bowled over by the *Eight Songs for a Mad King* and had invited us all to spend summer on the Adriatic island of Krk where she had an old stone house by the sea. Roy responded to her generosity by often focusing Rivers on her, held upstairs every afternoon when the outdoor heat was too strong.

was soon full, with about thirty people seated on low, cushioned stools and the others on the carpeted floor. Roy almost always sat in his high-backed swivel chair by the upright piano at the far end. There was often a collection of letters on or nearby the piano, and Roy would sometimes hand one to the writer and ask that it be read aloud. It might tell of a dream, a breakfast row, a sexual saga, a fantasy, a singing lesson, or an encounter with a parent. Comments were by Roy's invitation only, and if you had one you raised your hand.

Roy also gave sermons on death, life, art, language, relationships, sex, or music, inspired by some aspect of the letter, the look on a face, or sound of a voice. During these sermons he often linked seemingly unconnected things. He had developed a heightened, and often illogical, use of language which could be hard to follow in the way that poetry can sometimes be. He gave new names to old phenomena and demanded that we use the new term. For example, "a cold" was henceforth to be called "a warm," committees became "Life-fields," and to spend a night with someone was to "share a pillow" with them. As in his writing, he played with words and syllables and drew out unexpected meanings. He often commented on a look or a gesture and applied them to someone else's dream image from months ago, suddenly recalled, giving it new significance. He would ask us, "What am I thinking now?" and say, "Wrong!… Wrong again!… Yes, but why?" to our replies. Roy often railed against the "Pig Artist," or "Fartists," being those he judged as living only for their art or science and ignoring their bodies and their lives. "Einstein's theory of relativity establishes simply that the way in which you treated your wife last night affects the magnificence of your pure mathematical formulae. In other words, they are as impure as the way you treated her."[18]

Roy did not believe in accidents or coincidences, preferring to regard such events from the perspective of Jung's idea of "acausal synchronicity." Bodily symptoms, too, were put under the psychic magnifying glass. He had little sympathy for illness or poor health and followed a strenuous, daily physical and vocal exercise program and a careful, but carnivorous diet. He disliked vegetarianism. He was rarely sick, and I only once heard of him being unwell. One could feel quite guilty about having a cold—or rather "a warm"—and there was a

---

[18] From *Primer Acto.*

surprisingly low illness rate amongst the group during those years. He strongly recommended that heterosexual couples not have children. "There are more than enough in the world already, and our priority is to care for the newborn sounds in ourselves." He could be countered, though it was risky to try. Dorothy, his wife, was the most successful, although I do not recall him admitting to an error or to having forgotten something. It was fascinating to be there unless, of course, you had recently been attacked.

Occasionally Roy would refer to Wolfsohn, calling him "Awe." But for the most part, Roy was like other pioneers, rarely revealing his sources to us. Rather, one felt him to be both the author and authority on matters pertaining to the voice, body, and soul, that is to virtually all aspects of one's life. He was truly a "presiding presence," and many of us felt a dependence upon him for our growth. He attempted to offset this tendency by demanding us to give reasons for our affection. "Don't tell me you love me, tell me why," he often said. And he encouraged and provoked us to review our decisions to remain in his orbit. To those in doubt he would ask; "Do you really want to sing?" The word "sing" began to carry new meanings, including the indefinable experience of being close to oneself after a singing lesson, close to the essence of life. For me the thought of walking out on Roy felt suicidal.

Although he wove themes and words from his eclectic reading into our daily life, it seems obvious that, apart from Wolfsohn, the most important influence on Roy was Jung.[19] Jung's central idea of "the individuation process" lay behind much of Roy's attitude to the darker forces in the psyche; forces from which he sought to liberate us. Jung's idea also lay behind Roy's goal of re-educating the personality, and his commitment to inner revolution and authenticating one's motives. The paradox was that we were there to become individuals as much as to develop our voices or become actors. He once proclaimed, "I know of no name more worthy of my aspirations than that of Man."

Roy's words could be spoken with love, anger, sadness, and pleasure, and their utterance was always substantial, though not necessarily loud. His words were sometimes mingled with irony, confidence, or humour so one always had a sense of his being both a teacher and an actor. This was part of his "care-ful-ness," the way he sought to connect

---

[19] Was not Hart's choice of a god, Abraxas, only made possible through Jung's work, who wrote the *Seven Sermons for the Dead* in Abraxas' honour?

life and dreams by means of theatre—to make life into theatre. For example, if someone in a River needed to leave the room, and he or she did so in a way that broke the atmosphere, such as by leaving as quickly and unobtrusively as possible, that person would be called back and asked to return to his or her place. That person would then be told to try leaving again, but this time as a theatrical expression, doing so as much as possible in awareness of the energy and the musical phrase being made. This way we learned to see that behind the first exit lay a "disconnected mindscape."

For a time even coughing got the spotlight. When and how we coughed were closely scrutinised, and we were often found lacking in our dramatic and musical awareness. "If you must scratch your ear, do so consciously Noach" I was once admonished. Roy's view was that there should be no offstage behaviour because there is no "off-stage."[20] Roy's attacks were another part of his "care-ful-ness." He wrote: "My attacks on you are designed to bring you back to that point at your life at which you stopped growing."[21]

Roy also instituted rituals. For example, if a member of the group had to leave a River to go to work in the Club, he or she made an "Alhambra" at the door. This was a seriously executed but improvised *revérance*, a kind of florid bowing with feathered hat in hand performed by cavaliers in films such as *Robin Hood*. He took the name from the famous Arabic palace in Grenada, Spain, which had strongly impressed him on a visit there.

AND

Early in 1972 Rivers gave way to rehearsals for a new performance we called *AND*. This seemingly simple name was intended to invoke larger ideas that Roy and the group had been developing. The program

---

[20] I sometimes found all this excruciating coming from a background with such virtues as not "showing off," the unacknowledgement and non-expression of feelings among men, and disdain for any form of "affectation" or "mannerism" deemed to come from the "upper classes." But it was part of the work I was now committed to that went on in the singing lessons, rehearsals, and daily life. I was gradually being brought to face my own messy psychological reality and to take responsibility for changing it.

[21] From a letter to Marita Günther, referring to everyone in the group, dated 1974, Roy Hart Theatre Archives, Malérargues, France.

described it thus: "It is not acting in the sense of 'illusion' but of containing the overflowing cup of God 'and' the Devil." The title was that three letter everyday word linking those two mighty opposites, and it pointed to the middle ground of Abraxas. The sixteen core performers wore simple costumes and went with bare feet. For many people *AND* was the definitive Roy Hart Theatre performance, one without precedence and rooted in nonverbal vocal expression. Most of the words the performance did contain were sung, not spoken. The French press perceived it as a new form, naming it *le théâtre du cri*,[22] though the British press ignored it.

In other ways *AND* was a watershed in the history of Roy Hart Theatre. It was the first performance to tour in Europe and the first to be created by members of the group while Roy played only a supervisory role. Different sections were directed by Dorothy Hart, Vivienne Young, Robert Harvey, Richard Armstrong, Barry Coghlan, and others. In fact Roy was not even present at performances in Barcelona, Madrid, Bilbao, and Bordeaux. The press responded to the group's use of voice, gesture, and sense of ritual:

> ...a score of people whom one dares not call actors, though actually they practice the art of the stage perfectly. Is this experimental or laboratory theatre? Ritual would seem to be more correct.... —*Sud-Ouest*, March 30, 1972

> The work is admirable in its dedication. It is also a return to the beginnings; making theatre out of personal experience within the group, as doubtless occurred with those mysteries and rites that were at the origin of theatre.
> —*Gaceta del Norte*, April 13, 1972

> Have we ever cried out like this? We could have done it, once.... —*Informaciones*, April 11, 1972

> Before hearing these actors, it is difficult to imagine the range and diversity of the cry though the field of song and noise are also entered...if you are not subject to headaches this performance will astonish you.
> —*Le Courrier de Genève*, April 28, 1972

---

[22] "*Cri*" refers to a wider range of sounds than either the English "cry" or "scream," though both are contained in it; perhaps "cry out" is the closest translation.

> The *théâtre du cri* never ceases to use gesture. The whole
> body works, led by the sound. Each actor is capable of
> gymnastic performances, the ensemble sometimes achieving a
> remarkable visual harmony.
>
> —*Tribune de Genève,* April 28, 1972

The highlight of the *AND* tour was undoubtedly in Paris when Jean-Louis Barrault, the celebrated stage and film actor known for his role in Jean Cocteau's *Les Enfants du Paradis*, invited the group to participate in *Le Théâtre des Nations*, a ten day international event at the Théâtre Récamier in the *quartier* St. Michel. At this performance, Roy joined the cast, which had been enlarged to twenty-one members, including myself. The performance began with the premier of *Biodrame*, a dramatic poem for "multiple voices," written as a solo for Roy by Serge Béhar, a French poet, author, playwright, medical doctor, and a friend of Roy's whom he felt was the first established artist who comprehended Roy's work.[23] *Biodrame* can be appreciated as a metaphor for the second birth—that of the soul born within and through consciousness of the roles, interactions, and politics of the organs of the body, as well as giving insight into Roy's vision of acting. Coached by Dominique Deschamps, a young French literature graduate who had recently joined the group, "[Hart] performed in impeccable and well-educated French."[24]

But the audience response to *AND* was not what some expected, and the group was booed and heckled while on stage. According to Janet Harris (now Clara Silber, a graduate in biology who had recently joined the group), "Dorothy Hart was extraordinary in the singing lesson that she gave herself. She sang, 'I love my body' with increasing vigour and conviction as the booing intensified. She was standing in an open *plié*, hands on her thighs, looking beautiful and

---

[23] Béhar's understanding of Hart's political philosophy pleased him and he wrote in a commentary on the poem: "*"L'inegalité"* is the first political statement—a direct reflection of the sense of hierarchy between the head and body, the visceral and intellectual functions which influence each other, but which need theatre in order to become complete in a creative synthesis of the extremes—thus nerves are necessary for they put the artist's body into a state of wakefulness." The whole text of *Biodrame*, together with a commentary by Roy Hart, was published in *Roy Hart Theatre Journal*, Issue #4.

[24] *Nouvelles Valaisian,* Nov. 18, 1972.

strong; a wild woman in the truest sense."[25] It was later discovered that several of the hecklers at *AND* were members of Peter Brook's recently formed Paris company, also ostensibly engaged in pre-verbal researches.

AND provoked two critical articles which offered different impressions of the performance. The first was by Jean-Jacques Gautier, a long-established drama critic of the conservative daily, *Le Figaro,* who felt that the "cup" had far too much of the "Devil" in it.

> These rather attractive looking boys and girls seem perfectly convinced of what they are accomplishing. Their technique is faultless; the manner in which the work evolves is superb; the positioning, the production in all details, the staging, the attention to setting and focus of awareness, are simply admirable....
>
> But it is a ballet of animals.... As if the 1972 humanist ideal, the ideal of all those who claim to be members of the intelligentsia, and to have sensibility, art and culture, was to return to the level of beast and madman. Because what I saw there is what one can see and hear every day in the cages of the zoo; it is also that which, for a long time now, we deliberately do not do at St. Anne's, [a well-known Paris mental hospital].
>
> Firstly, I think about what this reveals *à propos* the idea one has of man. I consider then how this implies derision and hatred for human expression, for the word, language, the letter, text, ordered craftsmanship, the work of the spirit. I consider finally that I like innovation, if it brings growth, if it elevates the soul, if it contributes something, if it transcends man. But not this abasement.[26]

Unlike other times the group received had unfavourable reviews, this critic received a reply. It was written to Gautier by Janet Harris and later appeared in the first *Roy Hart Theatre Journal.* She rejected his view of the performance, stating that he did not stay to see how the audience reacted to the end of the performance:

> Two-thirds of the way through the performance Gautier left. His exit caused a stir in the audience, many of whom

---

[25] From a private letter dated 1997, in the author's papers.

[26] *Le Figaro*, April 19, 1972.

clapped. A clap, presumably of approval from sympathisers in the audience, who thought that they did not like what they saw or heard, and, like Jean-Jacques Gautier, wanted to depart. But they stayed and mocked and shouted abuse….[27]

José Monleon, in dealing with similar comments the previous year in Madrid, also came to Roy's defense:

> Because of the value Hart places on the voice some say his work is a kind of regression, belittling the importance of language and vocabulary. Others are apprehensive about the dangers of releasing repressed violence. They say that Man should be "split" between angel and demon, with reason and language as sentinels…the idea of a "total" investigation of man is irrational, as voices and shouts should be irrational modes of expression belonging to strong or painful real life situations.
>
> This is absurdly confused as the idea of "doing away with the mask," which is important to many modern theories of theatre, is confused with that of "doing away with reason."[28]

The second article *AND* inspired, by Catherine Clément, appeared a month later. Although she was there the same evening as Gautier, it was as if she saw a different performance. Clément, a trained psychoanalyst and writer known for her work, *Opera, or the Undoing of Women*,[29] was moved by the performance.

> Last night's performance won me over. I found it clear and familiar and perfectly constructed. The wild beasts, the baby, the lost child, the eagle and the dancers and all which speaks beneath the level of verbal language; it is like opera, like Wilson's *Deaf Man's Glance*. But one is more touched because of the voice and its hidden effects.[30]

In an article entitled "Voice and Madness: The Echo of the Origins,"

---

[27] *Roy Hart Theatre Journal,* 1, London, April 1973.

[28] *op. cit.*

[29] A discussion of Opera as an often violent male fantasy of women, doomed to extinction.

[30] From a letter to Roy Hart dated April 19, 1972, Roy Hart Theatre Archives, Malérargues, France.

Clément described how the performance was stitched with psychology's thread.

> ... [T]hese excessive sounds, which produce in the spectator either a fascinated enjoyment or an extreme irritation, produce events, acts, engender myths; the cry becomes madness, the voice becomes the support of delirium, the performance becomes unbearable and the ideological space of represented theatre is broken.
>
> ... So one finds in the Roy Hart Theatre performance the myths or the significant forms of our culture: Handel's *Hallelujah Chorus* in classical choral form, and the myth of origins, rediscovered in all those situations where animality, so close, is at the same time assumed and rejected. This echo of the origins which makes itself felt before us, in the evocation of Freud's "horde," in the simulated presence of the new-born baby, in the loss which the child feels and in its deep distress, is at the meeting point of voice and myth: at the precise point where the voice alone, apparently liberated from the constraint of meaning, finds it on the Other Stage: in the presence of the unconscious.[31]

While Gautier fled to his typewriter after the performance to attempt to put things back in order, Clément saw and heard through the shock to *AND*'s mythical core.

Are You Being Served?

In the Club restaurant on Saturday evenings, Monty Crawford held supper cabarets with food and entertainment provided by members of the group. The entertainment was varied. I performed a three-page "surrealistic menu" from *Memoirs of a Shy Pornographer* by Kenneth Patchen and Mozart's aria, *Oh, Loveliness Beyond Compare*, a piece I had been working on with Lizzie. A few of us created a rock and blues band, with Margaret on piano, Hans and David on guitars, me on electric bass, and fifteen-year-old Jeremy Samuels on drums. With Richard Armstrong we sang *Ruby Tuesday, Hey Jude, Far Away,* and *Stormy Monday*. Others sang tunes from musicals or songs by

---

[31] *Lettres Françaises*, May 23, 1972.

Bob Dylan and Nina Simone. Roy did not attend these events, and
the audiences were small, consisting mainly of friends and family, and
occasionally a club member or local resident.[32]

However, the Abraxas restaurant was packed when an unusual squash
match was offered to the public one Christmas. As ace player and Roy
Hart Theatre member Kevin Crawford recalls it, the event was sport-
turned-theatre in grand Monty Python style when he went head-to-head
with John Cleese:

> The match had been announced for some time: makeshift
> flyers and red-faced squash players spread the news. On
> Christmas Day, at midday, there was to be an extraordinary
> match between the Monty Python Yellow Dot team and the
> Abraxas Independents, culminating in a super-finale with John
> "Long shot" Cleese and Kevin "Crackers" Crawford.
>
> The preliminary competitions over, the two seeds finally
> faced each other before a packed and freezing gallery: half of
> Hampstead was on that balcony, and many a Christmas lunch
> was delayed by the marathon game that took place. Of course
> the match was the scene of some devilish psychological
> warfare, first declared by John Cleese, when he walked onto
> the bald court wearing no more than a ballet Tutu, white tights
> and the formal garland of a fairy godmother: but this was no
> godmother! It was a formidable human metronome, coming
> on court to tap the little black ball with a sickening regularity.
> Not to be outdone Crawford flounced on in his Nijinski garb,

---

[32] One of these was an attractive woman, another Angela, who had been a student
at Birmingham University at the same time as myself. There she was always in the
company of a group of wealthy Iraqi engineering students, and we had never said a
word to one another. Here, suddenly, I found myself invited to her flat across the road
from the Club for tea the next day. However, my secret fantasies of lustful nights were
drowned in a sleepless week of psychodramas as I discovered Angela to be psychotic.
My naive attempts to play the role of psychotherapist were only met with threats of
suicide whenever I tried to leave. Exhausted, I somehow extricated myself from the
situation, and Roy showed me an attitude of fatherly sympathy.

Another character from my past appeared one Saturday evening. This was "Snuggy"
Moores, the banjo playing, folk singing physics student whose off-beat company I had
so enjoyed as a teenager. He had now become a research astrophysicist, living in a flat
just around the corner from the Club. His invitation for a beer there only led me to
discover my inability to reconnect to those past times. I think I preached the gospel of
"singing" too much, and he was put off.

an ebullient sheharazade, timeless dancer pinning his opponent back with flowery winsome shots.

The game heated up, and the two players outshone each other in ingenuity and in improvised repartee. The audience hooted as Fairy Cleese lifted a Drawny arm to sink another smash: they howled when Satyr Crawford rolled on the floor in mock pain. Someone had been keeping score, and at last said it was all over. Neither player knew who had won, but it didn't matter as public and artists were convulsed with helpless laughter. Christmas lunches tasted better that year.[33]

However, the description of those lunches were certainly less Pythonesque than one recently announced in the Club restaurant which had been prepared and announced on the blackboard by Kozana Lucca, a new member of the group and a painter from Argentina. Lucca, who was learning English, brought an unusual flair to the lunch menu. One day she chalked up a lunch special as "ROOF BEASTS," referring to that traditional British fare, roast beef, and giving the members food for fantasy about what really went on up there on the top floor.

After a few months many of the regular members of the Abraxas Club—those who came merely to play squash and keep fit—grew weary of the group's antics around the building. Those who came in to have a good-natured game often met with a tearful group member along the corridor or intense looks on faces as Roy passed by. Those who came in to the restaurant for lunch often found themselves seated next to, and therefore overheard two group members turning their relationship inside out or some men in the group discussing the finer points of masturbation and the lone male psyche or the psychological origins of asthma. Going into the changing room could mean having to hear a dream being told under the shower. Bear hugs could be seen in virtually every part of the building, at any time of day or night, between any of the group members. Yet one may never know how much inspiration Monty Python,[34] whose regular membership to the Club gave them access to our group's dramas, later drew from such events and our voice workouts that inevitably seeped through the doors, walls, and corridors.

[33] Kevin Crawford, from an interview with the author.
[34] My attempts to question Mr. Cleese on the matter received a "too busy" reply. Could the Python have taken his first name from Monty Crawford, the Club's owner?

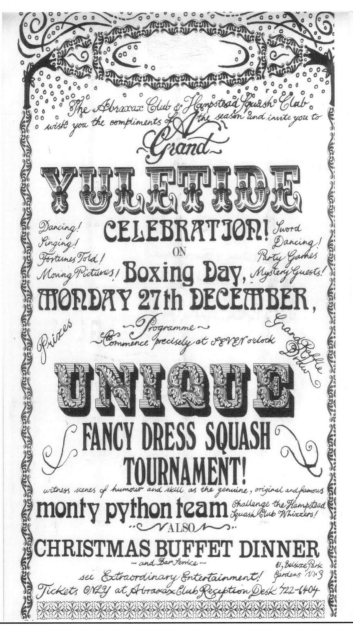

The announcement for the squash match with the Monty Python team.
Layout by Richard Armstrong.

It is perhaps for these reasons that the club was never successful financially. Monty Crawford often juggled money made from property investments, loans, and overdrafts, something for which he seemed to have a talent. He often seemed to take away wads of cash from the reception, leaving a bank deposit unfulfilled. He liked to dine in a nearby restaurant or go out on a shopping expedition for the Club. It was difficult, as his employee and cleaning man, to be polite and cooperative with Monty. He often gave conflicting orders, changed the place around needlessly every week or two, and was evasive and indirect when spoken to. But as much as he was a difficult person, so were many of us, myself included, and the Abraxas Club—infirm finances and all—became our nurturing "university" for six years.

The squash courts were also a source of friends from outside the group, and I first met Janet Harris on the court. As a recent member of the Club, she had suggested that we create a "squash evening" where players could meet and play in a relaxed and sociable atmosphere rather than the usual practice of arranging a game with someone privately. The idea was taken up and some of us who worked at the Club also joined in. Within a month Janet began to attend Rivers and then started to have singing lessons with Dorothy Hart. Janet and I both worked on the first *Roy Hart Theatre Journal*, which came out in April of 1973 and ran thirteen editions, ending in 1980. It was not long before our relationship expanded beyond the office, and we began "to share a pillow."

Love

In the early 60s, on assuming leadership of Wolfsohn's work, Roy had expressed his wish to be open about sexual relationships. Gradually sexuality became a central field of research for the group, not only in the abstract sense of dreams and symbols, but more directly, in the daily—and nightly—experiences of our relationships. Roy guided our relationships by asking us, "What is sex trying to teach us?" Our relationships were framed in Roy's idea that, "we are only on loan to each other."[35] But it would be wrong to imagine that the

---

[35] This frame owes much to C. G. Jung who, speaking of the nature of symbols with illustrative references to the phallus, then continues, "That which underlies all of these images—and sexuality itself—is an archetypal content that is hard to grasp...." From *Modern Man in Search of a Soul*.

atmosphere in the group was a permissive one. Initially heterosexual relationships within the group were generally long-standing and exclusive. The few homosexuals in the group went without male partners, because at the time, Roy, like Jung, believed homosexual practice to be abnormal. Roy even believed that through singing, homosexuals could be eventually rendered heterosexual.

By the early 70s Roy's perspective on homosexual relationships had widened. Richard Armstrong, who was bisexual at the time, told me that when he first came to the group, he found Roy homophobic, but that he later accepted homosexuality as a natural part of sexual and personal expression. Eventually, homosexual experiences within the group became an important phase in the "biological re-education of the personality." I am only aware of three long-term male members of the group who did not pass through them, if only for a few months (although there was only one lesbian relationship that I can recall). I too, went through this re-education with Barry Coghlan following a painful breakup with Janet. A dancer and group member, Barry would often come to the club early in the mornings to use the studio before Roy arrived, and the two of us would talk in the changing room or over a tea. Slowly I began to be open to the possibility of a relationship with Barry, and in early 1974, I began to spend one night a week with him. Although we made sexual contact at many of these meetings, the relationship had almost nothing to do with sex. For me it was about transforming my entrenched misogyny.

Of course many relationships, both homosexual and heterosexual, emerged during those years. For the most part these relationships were conducted on prearranged evenings of the week, and they were shared with the group. When a new relationship began, there was often a ritual performed in the studio in which the couple asked Roy and the group for their blessings. Uncoupling tended to be more discreet, although a breakup could surface during a River. No doubt many in the group suffered considerably as feelings of jealousy were worked through in the open, and much self-control and group discipline were needed to contain the problems that multiple relationships released.

Like Jung, Roy viewed relationships to be an essential vessel within which psychic transformation could take place.[36] But Roy believed the inverse was also true, that through a continual effort to bring care and consciousness into a relationship, individuation—which was Roy's primary concern—would be furthered. For instance, meetings between individuals, sexual or otherwise, were to take place by invitation only— one did not just turn up or walk into someone else's room. Roy believed that four "people" were actually present in the conscious relationship of a couple, by which he meant that beyond the biological level lies the psychological where each member has unconscious expectations and fears, in the form of projections and transference onto the other. Only when the relationship is conducted as an enquiry into this level, "in a spirit of cooperation and not competition," wrote Roy, "do we have the couple in the most sacred sense of the word."[37] How this theory actually worked in his own relationships is a matter for reflection. Roy's wife, Dorothy, wrote a poem called "Autobahn" in which she gives us some insight.

> We saw in a restaurant today
> At a table for two
> (so romantic an offer this gives)
> Facing each other in misery
> A man and a woman
> Aging, wizened, thin
> Their faces lined and sunken in
> With years of wrong unmusic.
> Lifetimes of uninformed abstention
> Morality gone miserly, mute-mad;
> It made us very sad
> It made us very
> Glad.
> It made us very sad,
> I said—
> "I'd like to wrap a coat of love
> Around that poor man's shoulders
> And watch him warm,
> His eyes grow wide
> With a new wild hope

---

[36] "There is no possibility of individuation on the top of Mount Everest where you are sure that nobody will ever bother you. Individuation always means relationship." C. G. Jung, *The Visions Seminars* (Zürich: Spring Publications, 1976), 506.

[37] From *Primer Acto*.

A broad belief in miracles.
But No,
I think he'd only close his eyes
And freeze
Conditioned to dis-ease."
And so
We turned to go
And ran
Into the cider-sun
Imbued
With a new-deepened gratitude.[38]

Paul Silber sees the marriage between Roy and Dorothy as an achievement of theatre:

> For twenty years, the couple remained loving to each other and
> lovers to each other. Anybody who has observed, even suc-
> cessful marriages, knows that such an accomplishment cannot
> be taken lightly. In Roy and Dorothy's case it was achieved
> through theatre. Unlike most lovers, Roy was not concerned
> with spontaneity. He was concerned with the apparent mainte-
> nance of spontaneity through theatre. This meant that at times
> he would consciously choose a course of action which had he
> relied on his spontaneity might not have occurred. And I be-
> lieve that there are many women—and for that matter many
> men who would prefer consistent warmth on an
> unspontaneous but conscious basis than occasional spontane-
> ous warmth. That Roy was able to maintain this consistency
> was due to theatre.[39]

Richard Armstrong believes Dorothy's challenges kept Roy's theory grounded in the daily give and take of their relationship:

> The way Roy kept his feet on the ground on a daily basis had
> much to do with Dorothy. She would pummel him, shout at
> him on the phone in the middle of a lesson she was giving.
> She wouldn't let him get away with much! For all her idio-
> syncrasies, the fact is she was an extremely normal, likeable,
> attractive, provocative woman, who was often the voice of
> common sense.[40]

---

[38] *Roy Hart Theatre Journal*, vol. 1, February 16, 1973.
[39] From "Who is Roy Hart?" a privately printed essay by Paul Silber.

When Roy Hart met Dorothy Stuart Findlay, he met a remarkable woman. She was born in Kenya on May 8, 1926, the youngest of four girls whose parents owned and operated a coffee plantation. All four girls were educated in England, and later Dorothy studied English at Cambridge University. According to Linda Wise, her niece and a member of the group, she was an unusual person from the start.

> …[A]fter the war she returned to Kenya to live with her mother. She was known to be very wild, gay, lively, very popular and had some difficult experiences with men. There was a colonel from the Kenyan Army living in the house who is said to have been very smitten with her and tried to seduce her. My first memory of her is from this time when she did a Spanish dance in a wonderful red dress and sang at the grand piano in the drawing room.

Dorothy, it seems, was not satisfied with conventional, European men. Early on she fell in love with Kidaha, the chief of a Tanzanian tribe of more than three million people. Kidaha, who had converted to Catholicism, had lost his position as head of the tribe due to his role in his country's fight for independence (although he is now the official tribal chief). Initially, Dorothy and Kidaha planned to marry, but plans were foiled because she was not a Catholic. Pregnant with his child, Dorothy returned to England and tried desperately to become a Catholic—even appealing to the Pope—but to no avail. A marriage between Dorothy and Kidaha did not take place.

As an unmarried white woman, pregnant by an absent African, Dorothy was rejected in 1957 Britain. Her family disowned her (though her mother later gave her the house at 21, The Ridgeway), and the lack of care she experienced on both medical and emotional levels was appalling. Complications from a swab left in her body after the birth left her ill, and she almost died. Now a single mother, Dorothy found a cheap room in Golders Green to rent. The man who opened the front door was Roy Hart. It was not long before the two were married.[41]

Dorothy was also tolerant of Roy's experiments in love. In the early 70s, at her request, Roy began to "share a pillow" with Vivienne, a rela-

---

[40] From an interview with the author.
[41] Paul Silber, from an interview with with the author.

tionship he began by asking the group if there were any objections. Although I recall none, there were repercussions. Alan Codd, a former lover of Vivienne's, was so jealous that he slipped into a near catatonic state, and shortly later, left the group. Dorothy coped with her jealousy rather more audibly, gaining a respectful reputation for intensive saucepan bashing sessions in her kitchen. A few months later she started a relationship with Paul Silber.

It was shortly after Roy began his relationship with Vivienne that he issued a decree that no couple should spend seven nights a week together and that everyone was to spend at least one night per week alone. This provoked turmoil, as many of the group sought to locate which bedroom might be free to be alone in and on which night. Richard Armstrong later told me that he considers this event, in combination with Roy's relationship to Vivienne and coping with Dorothy's jealousy, as a kind of watershed where things began to go awry.

"Phase Two"

In 1973 Roy instigated a number of other changes which were to transform both the nature of the group and the context of our lives. He referred to the changes as "Phase Two." His decision to perform with the Roy Hart Theatre was a major one. Through his solo performances, Roy had shocked the world with his radical new form of multi-octave vocal expression. This shock, enhanced by performances of the group which bore his name, was gaining the international recognition for the work that both Wolfsohn and he had so long sought. It was now time, he felt, to withdraw from his role as therapist and singing teacher and devote maximum time and energy to "the man of theatre" he felt he fundamentally was.

This would prove to be a difficult task. Roy had broken all contact with the three composers who had collaborated with him, breakdowns he accredited to his own sense of morality. In a letter dated December, 17, 1974, to Serge Béhar, Roy wrote, "Funnily enough, as for instance in *Versuch Über Schweine* or *Eight Songs for a Mad King*, when it seems that I am going to be allowed, so to speak, to continue the daily bread of performance, morality…makes that which I want—i.e. performance— disappear." Later Roy began to define "Phase Two" as having "everything to do with innocence and sinfulness. We are committed to finding out what is going on, by raising immorality to the highest level."[42]

Although in Rivers he praised the need for hypocrisy and compromise (which he renamed "with-promise"), in service to the greater "Thou" of art and relationships, he displayed little of these qualities in his dealings with composers. More composers might have written for Roy had he been less challenging to work with.

Roy had more in store for us. From being director of the text-based *Bacchae* in 1969, to a soloist who performed prior to the group-directed, almost nonverbal *AND* in 1972, Roy came to the centre by acting the lead roles in two scripted plays. "Phase Two" was also to be a return to the word. In a letter to a French television director, Roy wrote, "We have not outgrown the cry, which we have been practising for over twenty-five years, but on the contrary, we have absorbed it into every fibre of our being. For us, therefore, the word, philosophy, must remain paramount." The last performance of *AND* was in Tunis, a venue which touched Roy because of the Arab/Jewish question, and shortly after he sent statements to us in London hinting at what else he meant by "Phase Two."

> 1. We were invited to Tunis (Berlin). We accepted—performed—gave workshops. 2. After 25 years, we have completed the first stage. What will the second stage be? 3. Subjectivity is the fuel for objectivity. 4. Man's desire to be alone with his anima has, at last, suffered a reversal. The Jew has been forced to befriend the Arab.

The new phase included daily readings of well-known works, from *King Lear* to *The Elephant Man*, from the writings of Noel Coward to Oscar Wilde. There was also *Masque & Portrait*, a poetic *hörspiel* ostensibly in English, that began: "Hest dapone aver…" and continued with about seven thousand more words drawn from arcane, legal, and other obscure vocabularies.[43] Since it suited his purpose, Roy took up the challenge of this piece. For some weeks about twelve of us gave this seemingly meaningless sequence of writing soul based on Roy's ability to be "a man that could transport you by reading a page from the telephone

---

[42] From a letter from Margaret Pikes, Roy Hart Theatre Archives, Malérargues.

[43] I introduced Hart to the work's Australian author, Christopher Mann (now one of his country's established poets), who claims descent from the German writer, Thomas Mann.

directory."[44] *Masque & Portrait* was soon followed by a play in French by
Serge Béhar called *Mariage de Lux*.

A few months later, in March 1973, a German play written for the
Roy Hart Theatre arrived. *Ich Bin* was written by Paul Pörtner, who
spent some weeks in 1973 working and studying with Roy in London.[45] Although the group had not completed work on *Mariage de Lux*,
Roy announced that "we will go forward on all fronts," meaning we
would work on both plays at the same time. This was not an easy task.
Both works involved learning many lines and their meanings, choral music
and choreographed group movement over many months of intensive
effort. The chorus rehearsals, in which I was involved, were led by those
who directed sections of *AND* while Roy would work separately with a
small inner circle of the other characters, mostly played by those with
some previous professional stage experience.

In moving into the new phase, Roy demanded of the group a new
level of commitment and engagement. The casts of these two plays
were called on frequently to rehearse during the weekdays. We were
instructed to leave all personal matters outside the door, and we reduced
the few precious work hours we had to earn income. The rest of the
group's waking time, when not actually rehearsing, was spent learning in
one form or another. "Phase Two" turned the Abraxas Club into a
veritable academy. A typical day could involve French and German
tuition and homework, learning texts, ballet and contemporary dance
classes, choir practice on a passage from Stravinsky's *Symphony of Psalms*,
and a drawing class with Vivienne. This was in addition to three new
activities Roy had devised for us.

The first new activity was given the name *Cathédrale* and was a more
concentrated form of the cabarets that had been presented in the Club
restaurant. These new occasions took place in the converted garage
adjoining the club, which Monty Crawford—renamed Davide—had
recently managed to acquire. Roy named a director for each *Cathédrale*
who chose for it the name of a French cathedral town and attempted to
create a collage out of the various items offered to him or her by other
members of the group. These events provided a chance to develop

---

[44] *24 Heures*, Lausanne, 8 November 1972.
[45] Paul Pörtner, writer of plays, novels, and poems, was awarded the Zürich Prize for
Literature in December 1972. He was then working on a novel entitled *The Second Birth*.

skills in directing and an opportunity for individuals to share progress and innovation in creative expression in front of an audience.

Secondly, there was the training of new singing teachers through the creation of a teacher's "Life-Field," which was a forum to supervise and support teachers. Roy always maintained veto power over teachers, a control he sometimes used when he felt a teacher had gone wrong. Roy's gradual withdrawal from the roles of therapist and singing teacher in favour of performance meant that most of that therapeutic role of his work was now in the hands of a selected group of members. In this shift a new role of "talking teacher" emerged who was a different person from the "singing teacher." Others of us also began to teach singing and were given newer arrivals to the group as our first pupils. Mine was a flamboyant, Rudolf Nureyev impersonator from Eastern Europe who could usually be found around the changing rooms and sauna. Another early pupil was Vicente Fuentes, a former Catholic seminarist from the Canary Islands who had become a professional actor in Madrid. He had joined the Roy Hart Theatre on a one year scholarship but stayed fifteen years.

The third new activity was the creation of an Abraxas Workshop, which was open to the public. On three mornings a week, Akhmatova Samuels, Rossignol, and other teachers took over one of the squash courts to teach people outside the group. Several new members of the ever expanding group came through this channel.

Mixed Reviews

By Autumn, 1973, Roy felt there was sufficient material ready from the two plays, together with his solo *Biodrame*, to be put before the public as work in progress. A sequence of scenes, some even overlapping, were presented at London's Cockpit Theatre by a cast wearing mostly black "movement clothes." James Roose-Evans, a theatre director and writer who lived near the Abraxas Club and who had attended several meetings and earlier performances, wrote a guarded review of the performance for *Plays and Players* in December of 1973:

> …in this performance they will, without warning, switch from
> French to German or English. To those who have command

of only one of these languages, the experience can be bewilder-
ing or puzzling, far more so than Peter Brook's use of an
entirely new language…. Certainly the RHT [Roy Hart Theatre]
is a phenomenon to be observed with care…. At their best
they have created a powerful and new kind of music.

It was six months before the pieces were presented again, this time
in London's avant-garde "The Open Space." This performance generated reviews, but now guarded words gave way to scathing remarks.
Even the most generous review, written by Eric Shorter in April of 1974
for the *Daily Telegraph*, left the reader suspicious of the performance.

> Of the company's discipline, vocal and mimetic, there can
> be no doubt. Of its energy, dedication and delight in its
> activities we may be equally sure. Its timing and intensity are
> often hypnotic and its exploration of the range of the human
> voice in song, scream or chant, is fascinating.
>
> But I wish I could see, beyond the display of technique,
> some theatrical advantage in reducing a strictly symbolic tale of
> a confused marriage with religious overtones to an affair of
> shouts and murmurs. One gropes for a meaning which words
> might have supplied, and when the words do come why do
> they have to be mainly foreign? I felt like screaming myself
> long before the end—screaming for a synopsis or, better still,
> an intelligible script.

Other reviewers were less circumspect. They berated the lack of
(English?) words and criticised the unique use of voice. In short, the
reviews were devastating:

> For lovers of dialogue there was little to listen to…the perfor-
> mance meant what ever you wanted it to mean.
> > —*Stage & Television Today*, April 11, 1974
>
> A pre-occupation with the scream.
> > —*Sunday Telegraph*, April 4, 1974
>
> [There was shock at] strained neck muscles.
> > —*Daily Telegraph*, April 7, 1974
>
> …Mr. Hart's vocal training is a form of rape.
> > —C. Lewsen, *The Times*, April 4, 1974

It's difficult to tell what's going on apart from the cruder emotions, which rather blunts the argument for pre-verbal language.
—*Evening Standard*, April 9, 1974

In spite of a year's work on "returning to the word," the impression on
London's critics was that Roy Hart Theatre was still in the pre-verbal
"cry." Audiences did not hear it as music, and they did not like it.

However we hardly gave these critics a thought, and although
the criticisms were printed in their entirety in the next issue of the *Roy
Hart Theatre Journal*, there were only two comments on them by David
Goldsworthy. "Being revolutionary, our work is bound to be condemned
by the experts. From whatever point of view I look at it I cannot even
imagine that the critics' judgement, that it was a truly terrible performance, is true."[46] We ignored the reviews because we were engaged on
our re-education, re-embodying language, developing and affirming the
artist and the human being in ourselves, which had been, after all, Roy's
intention for years. Roy viewed critics as projecting their own psyches
upon our work, and he did not change this perspective during "Phase
Two." He typically shrugged at bad reviews saying that, "in a hundred
spectators there is maybe one who feels fulfilled, who gives in completely. RHT [Roy Hart Theatre] does not go out to look for a public, it
waits for one. Its objective is to meet the person."[47] There may also have
been another reason why Roy ignored the London reviewers.

Leaving London

In the spring of 1973, Roy announced that we were going to leave
London. Although we did not know for sure where we were going,
we knew we were leaving Britain behind to intensify the work on ourselves, our voices, and to create performances, thereby further closing
the gap between life and theatre. Roy's reasons for wanting to leave may
have been linked to his unsuccessful battle with the British cultural
establishment—a fight that included several rejected attempts to be
heard on BBC radio and an angry letter to the director of the Edinburgh
Festival—and the enthusiasm his work was getting from Spain, France,
and Switzerland at the time.

---

[46] *Roy Hart Theatre Journal*, no. 7, October 1975.

[47] From *Primer Acto*.

Switzerland was Roy's first choice for a new location, but unlike the Swiss theatre and music community, Swiss authorities were not interested in our coming to live in their country. Eventually Roy decided to move the group to France. In August 1973 on returning from a group holiday in Greece, several subgroups hunted for a suitable property. Despite dogged searching, only a half ruined and abandoned *chateau* that had been a centre for the French *Résistance* during World War II merited further research. The name of the property was Malérargues, an isolated hamlet in the hills of the Cévennes about fifty miles northwest of Avignon.

The prospective move not only shook up the group, but Roy, too, was going through personal changes. Beginning in September, 1973, he spent increasingly longer periods in the Alpine chalet, mostly with a small, inner group working on the two plays. Occasionally, he was there on his own, something he was not known to do previously. Early in 1974, Paul Pörtner had organised a radio broadcast in Hamburg for Roy. Richard Armstrong, who was one of Roy's confidants, was invited to join him several days before the event. He recalls that Roy's behaviour had changed and that he had become somewhat morose.

> We stayed for three days in a place he liked and spent much of them walking up and down a mountain. He was getting quite paranoid and strange in a way. He told me all kinds of things: he talked about the twenty-one-year cycles that Wolfsohn had told him about, and that, at 42, he would "know." He talked a lot about death, and his succession; he described the group very viscerally, as a monster coming up from the ground that was going to take him over. He was not going to return to London. I said "yes"—in those days one said "yes" to everything—I was quite excited really. I asked "What are we going to do?" "We're just going to go from hotel to hotel, maybe back to the chalet." But by the afternoon he had changed his mind and said, "No, we'll have to go back; I forgot about Jonathan's [Dorothy's son] schooling." But he didn't want to go back. Like he was giving time to something in his soul. He shared a lot with me about Vivienne, strangely enough. He was crazy about her, and wanted to elope to South Africa with her.
>   I do think he contained an awful amount of suffering in feeling he had been rejected by Maxwell Davies, by Henze, by

> Stockhausen. Yes, he had to behave as if *he* was rejecting *them*,
> he had to contain his ego's disappointment with all that.[48]

Despite Richard Armstrong's observations, Roy outwardly seemed to be in control of what became an exceedingly complex and demanding situation. Once more Monty "Davide" Crawford called up his special skills and juggled bank accounts, several large donations by group members, lawyers, and the estate agent to overcome the formalities involved with moving to France. Plans were laid for a first team to go and begin clearing and renovation work. There was much to be done since the more than twenty bedrooms, several large rooms, a kitchen, and dining room were in a sorry state. When it rained the inside of the house was liberally sprinkled through a network of leaks in the roof, while silt was deposited in the corridors by a stream from the hillside that entered through the back door and flowed right through to the front door, a floor lower. Every night a family of bats did their upside-down act in a corridor with broken windows.

In July seven pioneers left Britain, to be followed at regular intervals by smaller groups, one of which included Marita Günther as spiritual elder. The plan was to have the move completed by early 1975. The choice of who went and when was determined by several factors. The possession of useful practical skills was important, but one's relationship to the cast was even more important, as was one's place in "the hierarchy" of the group. At the start of "Phase Two," our place in the "hierarchy" was established since we had each been asked to represent our place graphically, the results being subsequently shown to the other members of the group, and our often incredulous and hurt reactions digested. I believe Roy wanted to minimise any illusions we may have had about our "status" in the emerging society before anyone left Britain.

Over the next eight months nearly fifty people from fifteen countries with diverse backgrounds and education gave up their jobs or schooling, sold their homes, furniture, and cars, and left London for an economically depressed region of southern France. There was no doubt in my mind that we were going in the right direction, and most were enthusiastic about leaving Britain for warmer lands. Despite the

---

[48] Richard Armstrong, from an interview with the author.

momentum gathering behind the move, Roy was not blind to the risks. In an interview on Radio London he said, "One translation of *Malérargues* is 'dangerous waters'—I hope that it will not prove to be so."

A short letter from a member of the group published in the fourth issue of *Roy Hart Theatre Journal* summarises the demands—physical, emotional, and financial—many of us were experiencing during the move.

> Dear Roy,
>
> The password is "contract," for you are seeking to renew your contract with each and every one of us, before Malérargues, and the way in which this will be done varies with each one of us…
>
> I also remember how you once stated that we must become smaller in order to become bigger. Another word for "become smaller" is "contract." The implications of this state-ment are that the alternative to "contracting" is *more* people *further* away from the centre. I don't think any of us want Roy Hart Theatre to be like that, so to keep our contract we must contract.
>
> There are only these two alternatives, of which I have indicated that only one is possible. Stasis is not.
>
> *Mais oui, vous verrez c'est inimaginable, ce qu'on peut faire avec les restes, les chutes, les dechets, la crasse.* ("But yes, you see, it's unimaginable what one can do with leftovers, droppings, waste, filth.") Serge Béhar has written one of the statements on which this theatre is founded, a statement of hope for all who work.
>
> Love, from Terence.

These contracts were not written documents but moral agreements and spoken understandings. Contracts were part of what we called *La Vision* and helped the thirty of us remaining in London to cope with the move. As jobs and homes were abandoned, there was a need to create a transitional safety net for the provision of basic needs. The Club served as home for some while others nested in the hallway of a flat. We organised ourselves into what was in essence a multi-skilled agency offering anything from Spanish lessons to baby-sitting to create a pool of income. Vicente Fuentes, for example, charmed his way into many local private gardens posing as an experienced Spanish rose pruner, working wonders with his voice and accent, though I suspect that the following spring's display was not so wonderful.

As a part of their contract, other members of the group contributed money to help finance the move. Davide's former wife, Kevin Crawford's mother, gave large sums of money under Roy's encouragement. Enrique Pardo and Terence Dunne, both relative newcomers to the group, gave parts of inheritances, while Paul and Nadine Silber contributed large amounts from the sale of their house. Although the contracts were not written, Roy imposed harsh requirements on certain group members. Louis Frenkel was asked to sever his business connections and donate the capital he would realize from doing so. It came as a blow when Roy heard from Frenkel that he could not accept Roy's conditions and that he would not be joining the group in France. Although Roy shocked us by shedding tears, he did not relent on the condition, and Frenkel, after fourteen years as a friend and one of Roy's financial helpers, was gone.

Roy made financial demands even on those who had little to spare. All group members were told they could not bring more than two tea chests full of belongings. What could not fit in the chests was sold, and the proceeds put into the group's fund. Individual money was controlled, and each household received a weekly food and expense allowance. Contracts often contained many details, some specific and some applying to everyone. Many of these details were worked out in Rivers, where Roy made it clear that the move to Malérargues would be no holiday.

And *La Vision* worked, although jealousy about who had to go gardening, who was sent next to Malérargues, and who got to spend time with Roy in the studio did surface. Roy's reply, in one River was, "Jealousy is what singing is all about." Perhaps to counter some jealousies, Roy told us no one was to consider the room they were to inhabit upon arrival at Malérargues as their own. "All rooms are Coco's room," Roy said. Coco Samuels was an electrician who had been associated with the group for several years. His contract entailed sleeping in a hallway. Roy's statement may also have been his way of putting the last first.

Reports of Rivers from this period were always sent to the Malérargues group, and in the Abraxas Club at precisely 8 P.M. every evening, all group members, no matter where they were, paused, turned inwards, and made a "loving connection" with those in Malérargues. Those in France did the same towards London. This new ritual was named *recueillement*, meaning "contemplation." Many times regular Club members came into the restaurant for a drink to find the space peopled by still and silent figures, rather as in the castle of Sleeping Beauty before the Prince arrives. I suspect that such events had an adverse effect on the membership statistics.

During this time of upheaval, performance work was not shelved. On the contrary, the "return to the word" continued, and Roy Hart Theatre was to become a professional company. What Roy meant by "professional" emerged during preparations for the first tour of the French-based Roy Hart Theatre in May 1975. He decided to abandon *Ich Bin* and *Mariage de Lux,* but not author Serge Béhar, who had offered to write a new play. But the process did not go smoothly. In December, 1974, Roy, Vivienne, and members of the group in Malérargues who had participated in a reading of the new work, *Café de Flora,* expressed their disappointment to Béhar in a letter. It began in Roy's handwriting:

> Dear Serge,
>
> This is not a lecture. It is a love-letter, an informed love-letter. I say that because I know that at times it may sound like a lecture.... ....you wrote to London saying that you were writing a play for me and us, which would be ready in three months. Three months went by. Nothing. At that time, I asked Lucienne to phone you because I was full of despair. Why despair? It is only now that those who are closest to me are realising that when all the forces which made my being into a leader, a father-figure, and a psychologist—when all those forces are removed, what can be seen is that which has always been: I AM AN ACTOR; THAT IS TO SAY THAT PERFORMANCES ARE MY LIFE-BLOOD.... What you have written does not reflect that which can be expected from a doctor, who has a relationship with us.

The letter described three dreams Vivienne had following her read-through of the work. Then Roy continued:

> Dear Serge,
>
> Perfect murder can be committed by killing the most visible of organs, Hope. This is something which the medical profession has yet to learn. Vivienne was forced to re-direct the play unconsciously through her dreams, from the moment she read it. For us to be able to work on *Café de Flora,* we need

to consciously re-direct this play.

Since Béhar had previously told Roy that he would write him another play if he did not like this one, Roy included several pages of suggestions for changes. The play was subsequently rewritten over the next few weeks by Roy, members of the group, and Béhar, with long-distance exchanges between London, Paris, Anzère, and Malérargues. Roy renamed the play *L'Economiste*, a title which had little to do with the script but rather referred to Roy. As a group, our living and working context would all be part of an "economy" whose value to the world would eventually be reflected in monetary terms. To Roy all work was a form of "singing," and Marx's formula "from each according to his ability and to each according to his need" seemed to me to be close to being realised. This may have been Roy's most revolutionary move of all—beyond a change of geographical location, it was a move into social engineering, taking his concept of the group as a "synthetic family" to an ultimate expression.

Of course, there were more hurdles to jump. Davide was juggling the dwindling income at the Club and any surplus revenues from *La Vision* and sending money both to the group in Anzère and Malérargues. At the time England was in a period of financial recession, and the value of sterling dropped from an earlier high of 13FF to a low of 8FF. In recognition of the challenge we faced, I renamed *La Vision*, *L'Impossible*. There were power struggles among the Malérargues pioneers, now numbering twelve, and Marita Günther often found herself challenged in ways beyond her means to resolve. Relationships were also producing heat and sometimes generating fierce emotions. In Roy's case, jealousy grew between his two partners. Vivienne wanted to bear Roy's child, but Roy believed biological parenthood was incompatible with the needs of his work. The subject was a source of tension, as was her wish to bear his name.

My own arrival in Malérargues was on Christmas Eve. Six of us travelled by overnight train to Alès, a grim town once given over to coal mining. Once we arrived, we were collected by car to take us the remaining thirty kilometers. Our spirits brightened as we passed through the town of Anduze with its old grey stone houses, red-tiled roofs, and dilapidated shutters, and into the Cévennes hills. Once there, we branched off into the rocky valley of the Gardon river, heading left along its tributary, the Salendrinque, by a dirty old farmhouse at Thoiras in the direction of Lasalle. These names were known to us as many of the rooms in the Club had been recently christened with those of the villages and rivers surrounding Malérargues. A vast orchard spread out across the valley where suddenly, Coco our driver, slid up a side track through the acacia trees and came to a stop in front of a long, three-storied building with cement walls and grey shutters. On its front steps, a small group of the pioneers were waiting to hug, be hugged, and guide us into the rambling, damp, old building.

Next day we were shown around the property including several *dépendances*, formerly homes to donkeys, wintering orange trees, and doves. There was evidence of chestnut smoking, silk spinning, and a natural spring, the property's only water source. In the largest of these rooms, Ian Magilton was hard at work preparing a rehearsal space for *L'Economiste*. Beneath it several smaller rooms were soon to be painted, and when the removal lorry from London arrived with its numerous pianos, they would be transformed into singing studios. Once we settled in we went outdoors in the warm sunshine, and over a convivial Christmas lunch, we passed news and gossip.

My first six weeks were spent painting studios and helping with construction for water conservation, a major concern as there were doubts that the spring would keep up with the needs of fifty people during the dry summer months. Roy and his "tribe" from the mountains arrived in early February. With more arrivals from London, the crossing of the Red Sea was almost complete.

Living conditions were Spartan, and we shared rooms with little heating. Many of us had no personal money, and most of us had little freedom of movement, action, or thought outside the intensive regime necessary to renovate Malérargues and give birth to *L'Economiste*. Heide Hildebrand had been working on preparations for a tour in May, and several dates in Austria and Spain as well as a dress rehearsal in Alès were now fixed. There were to be no holds barred in making this, the first European based creation, into a successful Roy Hart Theatre performance. It seemed to us that now everything was at stake.

As work proceeded it became clear that Roy wanted the piece to be readily accessible to the public, and on one level the play functioned as a romance, in the style of a musical comedy, between Maurice, a philosopher/poet (Roy) and Flora (Vivienne), who has left her comfortable family background to run *le café du monde*. The text was in French, which few of us spoke well, though we worked hard on learning it. And there was a five piece dance band, in which I was the saxophonist. Roy also worked intensively on a daily basis, at first mostly with the other main characters, although the entire cast would take a morning movement class and re-meet in the evening with the whole group. Gradually others of the cast were brought into the rehearsals, and occasionally even members who were not.

One day while David Goldsworthy and I were busy cutting wood, Roy asked us to join him in the newly prepared Studio Theatre with our musical instruments. We gladly exchanged our axes for a guitar and a battered alto sax and entered the room, where he was working alone on some lines of *Maurice*. A cassette recorder was turned on when we played, and the result was later played to the group. There was an infernal echo effect from the hard walled room, but Roy was delighted with the recording and told Heide that copies should be sent out to the prospective theatres by way of a foretaste. Such moments, when I realised that Roy really needed us, made the rest bearable.

A division of labour had been established with specific individuals responsible for tasks such as cooking, cleaning, building, and renovating. New arrivals were quickly integrated into the system. At 8 A.M. and 6 P.M. each day, most of us gathered in a circle to hear *sonrisas*, statements of work needs for which we volunteered or to which we were assigned. The chateau had no sewage disposal system, and we began using Elsan camping toilets, nicknamed "El Cid." The daily ritual of tending them was deemed to be "men's work" and included digging a hole and emptying buckets into it. At a critical moment, Frank, who was in charge of the renovation work, showed a sign of doubt about the justice of this new economy. Within a few hours he was on his way back to London. Ian Magilton recalls:

> One evening Frank and I took our usual run down to the river to wash off the building dust, and walking back he expressed his disturbance at the sudden intensity of rehearsals—which was pretty violent. I felt sorry for Frank, that he

needed help, and that as usual his directness was possibly "on to something." At dinner those days, there was a kind of rotation system whereby one of us would get to sit next to Roy, and it was my turn. I had the impression that Frank was the most loved person of us all, so I spoke to Roy of his discomfort. Roy said that the situation we were in admitted to no defeatism and that Frank should return to London as soon as possible; I should tap a glass, stand up, and tell him so. I was shocked, that this was a death sentence, and that I had betrayed Frank's confidence. I tried to re-explain it to Roy and Dorothy, but he insisted. I have always thought it was a mistake, but riding the wild horse of Roy's madness, we were bound to make mistakes.[49]

The "new economy" was especially testing for those not in the cast. Roy was aware that he could be accused of their exploitation or manipulation, which was in part the reason for contracts. Others also recall a toughening in Roy's attitude once he was installed in Malérargues. Linda Wise, a niece of Dorothy Hart and one of the inner circle of *L'Economiste*, remembers that joy seemed to fade away from Roy's rehearsals.

In London I often met Roy and Vivienne in Davide's flat, next to the Club, and found him warm and friendly. I actually received several individual lessons from him. After the move his atmosphere changed, he became very ruthless. I think it was partly to do with Louis Frenkel's withdrawal. There was no pleasure in the rehearsals.[50]

Roy made his lack of joy known to us, if through indirect means. One morning Roy instructed us to walk rhythmically in twos in one large circle, a movement that filled the whole room, while chanting the phrase *jour après jour,* meaning "day after day." The line was from the conclusion of the marriage scene of *Maurice and Flora*. After about one and a half hours without pause, Barry was able to negotiate a change in direction, from which moment we continued for another hour and a half.

A Brutal Parting

---

[49] From an interview with the author.
[50] From an interview with the author.

However, even under these pressures, we did not remain totally cut off from local inhabitants. There was naturally some curiosity among the French locals about this large group from London recently arrived in their region. The previous exiles who came from that city, Charlie Watts of *The Rolling Stones* and family, had not stayed long, and in one of the most economically depressed areas of France, any potential stimulus to the economy was welcomed. Yet from the start it was primarily for our voices that we were welcomed and were afforded what transpired to be long-term credit by several local suppliers.

And it was our voices that cemented the relationship with the real estate agent through whom the chateau had been bought. He was invited to the inauguration of the Studio Theatre, which Ian had transformed from a large windowless workroom still bearing the traces of the silk spinning that had ceased in 1905. We had sung a *Gloria* there.

> One of our *Cévenol* friends who was there, Monsieur Daufès, the estate agent and a member of the *Résistance*, was moved by our voices and wanted to share his joy with other local people. That is how we were invited to sing hymns and choral pieces, such as Handel's *Hallelujah Chorus*, in the Protestant service of the small local church in Thoiras, and even though we are not a religious choir or community in the usual sense, we accepted this invitation because we believe that life is religious by nature and that human relationships are very important.[51]

The *Hallelujah Chorus* from *AND* and an original way of telling the Creation story, accompanied by a multi-octave choir, was received with curiosity by the mostly farming parishioners who heard us in several Protestant and Catholic churches. Such events were rare moments when the whole group, including Roy, left Malérargues, and it was during these performances that I began to see where we were now living. Some of these people made up the audience for the first presentation of *L'Economiste* in Alès. Some were shocked but most found in the play a substance which gave more solidity to that which they had already received in church. The performance provided an occasion for us to practice on a full-sized stage and to test our comprehensibility in French, even though the tour would take us to countries where French

---

[51] David Goldsworthy, *Roy Hart Theatre Journal*, no. 7, October 1975.

was not the mother tongue. Although there are no formal reviews, the performance must have gone well since two local residents, Jean-Jacques Court, a former Olympic hurdler, and Richard Bruston, a professional photographer, were impressed enough to make personal contact with some of us and were soon giving invaluable practical help and advice.

We left for Austria when the acacia buds were almost ready to burst open in a May display around the chateau. Heide had arranged things well, with time to rehearse and much needed time to relax between the performances. The latter became a theme in a River held one evening in the hostel where we were staying outside Vienna. Roy had heard that a small troop of us, including myself, had made a visit to the centre of Vienna and drunk a coffee there, and he asked the group if we were right in having done so. When the majority of hands indicated that we were wrong, my heart sank in a way I knew only too well. But I was rocketed skyward a second later when he emphatically told that majority, "Wrong! Of course they were right to go!" He also told me there, one evening after supper, that "You will soon be where you should be; close to me." There were to be other tender moments with Roy over the next few days, which I took to be signs of awareness and support of my relationship with Barry.

After a performance in the mountain town of Villach, I took a walk in the town. Close to the theatre, by the side of the rushing river, I heard Roy's voice gently call, "Richard." Seeing Richard was not near, I replied, "It's Noah." He was sitting alone at an outdoor café table and invited me for a drink. He told me that it was not a mistake that he had called me Richard, and subsequently repeated this to the group. For some time I had envied the privileged relationship Richard Armstrong had been afforded by Roy, and here in Villach, I sensed Roy to be indicating that in some way, I, too, was to enjoy such closeness in the future.

The performance in the Theatre Festival of Villach is the only one during the visit to Austria for which a review can be found. The writer's observations give the impression that while Roy's message got through the language barrier, she found in *L'Economiste* material for her feminism.

> ... The action is overflowing with depth psychological symbols. Even if one does not understand the words, one feels the archetypal shadows glide across the stage in certain scenes....
>
> The immense task which the company has given itself

with this piece, is to make a metaphysically universally valid and intelligible theatre for everyone. But in spite of magnificent individual performances (by Vivienne Young and several others) it fails formally because of the use of too many different means of expression. It fails in content because the underlying philosophy emphasises the male principle too strongly—in a time of laborious struggle for the establishment of partnership principles—which is linked to the over dominant position of Roy Hart as family head.[52]

Other fists were raised the next morning when we took part in a public discussion during which Roy was accused by some students of "leading a school for fascism." We were astonished having experienced no such reactions in the Cévennes, and we believed *L'Economiste* to be more accessible than the last London show. The bluntness of the students' statement made me realise how far I had come since my student days. Roy said that there was more to be learned from enemies than from friends, and listening to these students, I experienced exactly that. Another member of the group wrote "…every qualitative and disciplined artistic impulse is attacked through political argument. Even the relationship of actor with chorus, which constitutes the very foundation of theatre, was interpreted politically as that of a leader and the masses."[53] Uncharacteristically Roy was affected by the accusations.

The next performance was in Heide's hometown of Klagenfurt and

An outdoor River under an ancient olive tree on the island of Paxos, Greece, July 1973. Roy Hart is in the center, speaking.

[52] E. Darnhofer, *Kärtner Tageszeitung*, 10 May 1975.
[53] Enrique Pardo, *Roy Hart Theatre Journal*, no. 7, October 1975.

was given in the afternoon to an audience mainly of school children. Roy at one point gave an instruction to skip a section of the play. After the show I met him outside the theatre by his BMW in which he was to travel to Valencia for our next performance. I had come with my cumbersome handmade music stand and asked him if there was room for it in the boot but was politely refused. And after the recent implications of a new closeness with Roy, I felt hurt by my exclusion from the group he chose to stay with for a few days in a mountain chalet. Seizing the moment with him, I asked, "Roy, will I ever see the top of the mountain?" He replied, "You, of all people, my dear Noach, will see the top of the mountain." He turned away and climbed into his car.

Those were the last words Roy was ever to speak to me.

"The Magic Chord" in *AND*, 1971. Photo Ivan Midderigh.

CHAPTER SIX

Paul Silber Remembers[1]

18 May 1975

It was about 10 o'clock on a lovely spring morning in the month of May. It was the 18th May, and the year was 1975. Dorothy Hart had just had her 49th birthday 10 days before, on the 8th, and I had my 37th birthday just five days before, on the 13th. What a beautiful sunny day it was. Warm, warm enough for me to travel in the car wearing only my shorts. A very gentle wind was blowing in from the Mediterranean coast, not far from where we were, just inland from Nice. We packed up the bags and put them in the boot of the car, which with four people's luggage in it, was then completely full. It was a Sunday morning out of the tourist season, before even the real beginning of what now passes for tourism, on that vastly overestimated stretch of coast, even existed. There was nothing else moving on those roads at all on that beautiful sunny Sunday. So sunny and so warm was it that we decided that we would rather travel along with the sliding sunroof of the car wide open. We had, as usual, spent rather longer than was wise over our breakfast. This was because, as usual, we had to have an analysis of our dreams before setting off. I had had an amazing dream that night which Roy and Dorothy had entitled "The Phoenix Dream." How extraordinary, in the light of what was about to happen, that they interpreted the dream with that particular word. This was also the famous

---

[1] Editor's note: The following is an unedited account written by Paul Silber.

occasion when Roy, having heard the contents of all the letters coming from Malérargues, commented that "there are no leaders in Malérargues," and he said this with great sadness in his voice. As it turned out this was subsequently proven to be entirely true.

When we realized what time it was, there was something of an emergency on our hands. We still had to get all the way around the Mediterranean coast to Barcelona by nightfall. It was a Sunday, a very quiet Sunday in a very sleepy southern France, we had very little petrol left in the tank and we looked all around the town of Nice for an open petrol station, there were none. We drove on to the Auto-Route hoping there would be one open there, and after a while we found one. I had been driving the BMW 2.2 up until then, by now it was about 11:30 a.m. We filled up and we were about to re-enter the car to continue on our way, when Vivienne asked Roy, "Can I drive the car for a while now Roy?"

"Well, Paul, what have you to say about that?"

There was an inordinately long pause. Normally Roy would have commented on such a long pause as being bad theatre, but nothing, strange, very strange. In the absence of anything else being said, Roy then said, "Well then that's settled. Vivienne you will drive."

I felt strangely sad and put down. Vivienne got into the driving seat. There were very few minutes left.

We drove out of the petrol station and on to the Auto-Route, we started to pick up speed. The atmosphere in the car was calm, very calm, almost serene. Dorothy especially was happy and quiet, she was sitting next to me in the back, she was writing a letter to her family in Scotland. Roy was reading his book in the front with Vivienne. She was to his right as it was an English car. We began to take a very long slow turn to the left. Then we were moving at 130 km/h.

Vivienne turned to look at Roy. Then a very strange thing happened, Roy turned to look back at Vivienne. He would never have done such a thing normally. He would have immedi- ately said, "Concentrate Vivienne, keep your eyes on the road."

Nothing, strange, very strange.

How long did they look at each other? Three, four, five seconds? I don't know how long it lasted, it seemed to me a very long time. They were in love with each other, perhaps this is enough to explain everything that happened, I think not all of it however.

When Vivienne turned her eyes back to look on to the road she found that the car had been moving on in a straight line, the road, however, had been slowly turning to the left, the car was already on the hard shoulder, very near the edge of the Auto-Route. There was a row of little wooden pegs with red tops sticking up out of the soil in a line just off the Auto-Route's edge. Beyond this there was a field that was on the same level as the Auto-Route. Vivienne was not an experienced driver, she had only passed her driving test a few months before. Just the slightest easing of the wheels to the left would have been sufficient to correct the problem but no, she was surprised by the nearness of the edge. She gave the wheel a hard yank to the left and we started on our last journey. The car turned too hard to the left, Vivienne tried to correct it, turning to the right, too hard again. I don't know how many times we skidded first to the right and then to the left and then back again. It seemed to me that it was quite a few times. Roy had put his book down on his lap, he was looking straight in front of him, he had on his lips a strange little smile. He never, wisely, tried to give any help to Vivienne in her fight with the control of the car. I was sitting very upright, right between the two front seats holding on to the back of them, one with each of my hands. I was very tense, stiff even, with fear, these are facts which together came to save my life.

After the third or fourth attempted correction of the wild careering of the car had passed without any effect, the final stage that was to end everything, was already close at hand. The rear right-hand wheel collapsed, it folded in underneath itself, then there was nothing left that any of us could do anymore, it was all finished. The car started to spin around

to its left, the speed must still have been over 100 km/h. The
remaining three supporting wheels under the car were insufficient for it to remain upright. It turned over on its roof,
onto its beautiful sunshine roof and there it was, completely
friction-free. The car was able to spin around at great speed
about its own axis, like a spinning top, throwing all its contents
all over the road all around it.

I had been the first to be thrown out of the car. Because
of my central position in the body of the car, I had been
thrown out cleanly through the rear window, breaking it first
with the crown of my head. Fortunately I had passed out just
before all this was to happen whilst sitting inside the car. The
BMW 2.2 of that epoch was the first of its kind that had a big
enough back window to allow a human body to pass through
it. Even so, to do so at that speed, without hitting the spinning
metal cages (these were razor sharp) that were left there after
the rubber seal had been broken out, was already a miracle.
Poor Dorothy, she was not so lucky, she also was thrown out
of the back window of the car after me, but because she
was in the corner of the car, she was thrown out while turning
sideways through the air, hitting the metal edges of the window
as she went through it.

Roy and Vivienne? They had not been wearing their seat
belt, had they done so they might well be alive and well today.
The centrifugal force of the car spinning on its roof had
thrown them forward through the front window, unfortu-
nately their legs being under the dashboard of the car, these
were caught, their bodies were folded over the dashboard,
their heads having already broken through the front
windscreen, they were unable to be either thrown out clear
of the car's wreckage out on to the road, nor to remain intact
within the body of the car. They died from their stomach
wounds.

The last and the greatest of the miracles that saved me
that day was that at the moment when I was thrown out of
the car while it was spinning around upside-down, it happened
that the back end of the car was facing in the direction along

which the car had originally been moving in the first place. The speed of my ejection through the window was therefore slightly reduced in relation to the original speed of the car. I landed on the back of my poor head and on the top of my naked shoulders. It says something for the suppleness of my back that I was able to take up the speed of my movement by rolling over the glass strewn around, over and over, head over heels along the hard shoulder of the Auto-Route until I also came, at last, to a stop.

At this time I was completely unconscious. Somehow, even in the depths of my unconscious, I must have known something of what was going on. Something deep within me must have wanted, with a great need, to say my final goodbye to Roy and Dorothy for the last time. I partially came to for a few instants. In that state of consciousness, what I saw and felt before me was the following: Firstly that I was buried horizontally in the ground up to my neck (that must have been an indication of that amount of pain I was suffering). The second thing I saw was Roy. It seemed to me that he was lying on his side in a fetal position in the sand of a great desert. I could hear the gentle sound of the wind blowing. Behind him was a great boulder. It was calm, very calm, serenely calm. That was the last time I ever saw my dear sweet friend Dorothy Hart and my loving father Roy Hart.

Twenty four years later, I can unambiguously state that in all the years that have passed since their deaths no one and no thing has ever filled the vacuum in the world of theatre that their deaths left behind them.

I woke up that Sunday afternoon in an overheated hospital room pouring with sweat, the sunshine still pouring in through the window, having the skin under my left eye and under my nose being sewn up by a young doctor, who didn't know what to do with an even younger patient, who was supposed to be still asleep and certainly not supposed to be suffering any of the pain that I was suffering from. I was in the hospital for two days. It was in there that I learned for the first time consciously that Roy and Dorothy were indeed dead. It was both for me personally and for the world in general a very sad end of a very great epoch that was never to be replaced. On that day in May, the whole world of Western European culture took, along with Roy and Dorothy, a slow turn to the left, a turn out of the consciousness that Roy was proposing for THEATRE, and into the backwards spin of the safety of drawing room performance energy. One has only to look at the standard of acting in today's theatres to realize the truth of this.

Davide Crawford came and removed me from the care of the hospital two days later. Both the doctors and the nurses were very much against my being released. The Roy Hart Theatre could not afford for me to remain in the hospital any longer, thus greatly risking my future health. (Why either the car insurance and/or my English social security couldn't have covered the cost of all this, I will never know.) I remember one of the nurses on hearing the news told me, "It is not possible for you to leave the hospital now" and immediately she spun me around and picked out, causing me great pain, a piece of shattered glass from my back. I remember that I had to sign a paper that released the hospital from any medical liability in view of my untimely release from their care. It was true that for many months after that, little pieces of glass would emerge unexpectedly from my body at unexpected times and in unexpected places.

My journey from Nice back to Malérargues was the most macabre I have ever undertaken in my life. It took place in a little hired van, in it with me were the three plain wooden coffins containing the bodies of my three dead friends.

Within two weeks of my return to Malérargues, we were again rehearsing "L'Economiste." What possessed us to do this I cannot imagine. For us to have attempted to insert our own little selves into the places of those, our lost giants of theatre, was an act of the greatest possible folly. However this is what we insisted on doing. I remember that during the warm-ups in those early mornings, I would notice from day to day the strangest progression in the movement of a pain passing through my whole body. It would take a rhythm of three to four days in each place. It would start in my right elbow and pass through to my right shoulder, then it would go over to my left shoulder, then it would slide down to my left elbow. And then it would pass back to my left shoulder, then across to the right shoulder again, and so on and so on. In the end I went to a doctor and was prescribed a serum to be injected into my arm against tennis elbow, would you believe it? Interestingly, I had a dream at that moment in time in which I took the serum back to the doctor who had given it to me in the first place. In any event the treatment had absolutely no effect on me whatsoever. I can no longer remember any more when I first experienced that agony of my shoulder dislocating itself. But I have no doubt whatsoever that this was caused directly as a result of the car accident. Over the years since then, I have no idea how many times this dislocation recurred, but it was many times. Finally it came to such a point that it was so used to coming out of joint that even an act as simple as drawing a curtain back would allow it to come out, always with the same terrible agonizing pain. So, at last it was decided that the problem could be cured by an operation being performed on it. This was duly done in the Clinique of Ganges and after some re-education on it for a little time afterwards it became all right again. I have subsequently never had any trouble with it ever again.

As the time moves further and further away from the date of the accident, it becomes less and less sure whether the problems in my other joints were directly related to the accident or not. It seems quite possible, however, that these more recent weaknesses were also induced by the shock of the accident.

All that I have said above still cannot satisfactorily account for how I managed to survive the terrible forces at work in that accident. Clearly there must have also been forces at work that sunny day that can only be described as being those of a supernatural order. For myself, the miracle of my survival from that terrible accident in the face of all my friends' deaths, can be more than explained by the fullness of the life that I have been able to live since that time. I have found solace in the fact that many people have been personally helped and creatively guided by the voice work that was inspired by Roy Hart and was transmitted by myself and Clara, my wife, in the many workshops and performances that we have given in the twenty four years that have passed since that terrible day in May 1975.

The End

Paul Silber
1999, Malérargues, Thoiras, France

Only Silence

I was en route from Vienna to Barcelona that day with the rest of the cast of *L'Economiste*. A stop-over at a hotel in Nice had been pre-arranged, and it was there that we heard of the fatal accident, relayed to us from Malérargues. Apart from cries by myself and Vincente, there was almost no vocal reaction on hearing the news but instead only silence. Later that day I sat for hours with Barry on the pebbled beach beneath the *Promenade des Anglais* gazing out to sea, with the question, "Do I leave now?" slowly crystalising on the horizon. Many years later I discovered that this question arose in the minds of others, too.

To have answered "yes" would have been to agree with all those who had projected an image of fascist or guru onto Roy and of "docile followers" onto us. For me it seemed a denial of the years of struggle towards becoming an individual. For all of us, it would have been to abandon the "Idea" we had come to serve and love. In recent months Roy had hinted at some kind of a separation to come once the move from London was complete. He would not live in Malérargues but up on the hillside in a chalet already known as "Roy's Chalet," and his sadness at the lack of leaders among those now there was part of this picture.

But why so brutal a parting? What would become of us? Now was the moment of greatest peril, and Roy had been preparing us to face it. In the previous years he had more than once referred to his mortality. In 1971 he wrote to us all from abroad:

> If you hang on to each other it means that you are afraid to die, which you must…sometime, perhaps soon…this is not a morbid thought. It is a fact, live serenely in this knowledge, make every smile count, every tear a joyful encouragement, every gesture a healing one, in short be compassionate. Don't hang on—let go: and sing.
>
> The death I'm talking about must and does lead to life; because it implies control and discipline. The control and discipline I'm talking about means that death has no dominion, because I know that it is there, by my side, making me feel more, want more, live more.

Richard Armstrong (center) leads a rehearsal (from left) Pascale Ben, Diane
Palmer, Nadine Silber, Anna Allen, Dominique Deschamps around 1972;
photo by Ivan Midderigh.

Dorothy Hart, Kevin Crawford, and Roy Hart in 1972 in London at the *Barque and Bite* restaurant; photograph by Ivan Midderigh.

The first seven leave London for France.

Ich Bin (1973) Top: Vivienne Young and Roy Hart.
Below: Barry Coghlan, Richard Armstrong, Derek Rosen, Robert Harvey,
and Roy Hart. Photos by Ian Magilton.

The burial ceremony of Roy Hart, Dorothy Hart, and Vivienne Young,
23 May 1975, at Malérargues. Jonathan Hart plays piano and sings
with Dominique Deschamps a duet from *L'Economiste*.

Malérargues (1975). Photograph taken from behind and above the property.

AND—"The Magic Chord"—Théâtre des Nations, 1972
(photo Clara [Harris] Silber)

The Wolfsohn / Jung Letters

The following appendix consists of parts of the correspondence between Alfred Wolfsohn and C. G. Jung, most of which is held in the C. G. Jung section in the Scientific Archives of the ETH Bibliothek, Zürich.

I visited the Archives March 9, 1998 with Veronika Latini, a native German speaker fluent in English and a long-time reader of Jungian literature and archetypal psychology. At my suggestion Veronika first read through the complete correspondence as it was presented to us, with certain pieces absent. Her first and clear impression was that Alfred Wolfsohn addressed Jung as a knowledgeable, wise father, using a respectful tone, and with a strong and profound need to get his response. As the correspondence proceeds Alfred Wolfsohn becomes disappointed and saddened, though accepting.

Alfred Wolfsohn. Berlin. Sept. 27, 1937. Not made available to me by Dr. Hörni-Jung, acting on behalf of the Trustees of Jung's writings, because of "medical confidentiality." This was probably the letter referred to in Wolfsohn's manuscript, *Problem of Limitations*, which he had sent to Jung to accompany a dream he had of Jung and a classical "chamber" singer, Richard Tauber. The relevant part of the manuscript reads:

> In the accompanying letter, I said that the dream was my visiting card and also the reason for my desire for an interview. As the authority on dream interpretation, he should decide whether he considered this dream of sufficient importance to grant me that interview…[dream then recounted]…. Jung replied at once that he was expecting me at his hotel.

Alfred Wolfsohn. Berlin—Grunewald, Zikadenweg 39. (*Translator'*
note: This address is now in a well-known, pleasant, and affluent suburb which was
part of East Berlin) **Sept. 8, 1938.**

In this letter, Wolfsohn reminds Jung of a letter he had written him
a year before...

> [Y]ou had kindly agreed to a discussion at the time of
> your visit here. Because of several misunderstandings on the
> part of the management of the hotel in which you were
> staying, this talk fell by the wayside.
>
> Then, on the evening of your lecture, when I was briefly
> allowed to speak with you, you permitted me to write to you
> what I had wanted to discuss with you face to face. Because of
> this agreement, I send you this letter and also my manuscript
> (*Orpheus, or the Way to a Mask*) My personal conviction in
> taking this step is that the results of my work, coming from
> another field, can contribute to your research.
>
> It is very clear to me that the special aims which my book
> pursues do not allow me to delve into the treatment of details
> here. My most urgent wish is to report these details to you
> personally. Necessities imposed on me from the outside, on
> which I believe I do not have to elaborate, urge me to try every
> possible road to continue the work I have begun and to
> develop it!

Wolfsohn then asks Jung if, on the basis of Jung's reading of the
manuscript, it is important to have the discussion that did not take place
when Jung lectured in Berlin, concerning details Wolfsohn does not want
to write:

> ...can I count on this discussion with you in Switzerland?
> In this case it would be necessary that you send me a short
> invitation which points out very clearly the reasons for my
> journey.
>
> I have tried to express my gratitude towards you in the
> sense that I have tried to serve your work. If you happen to
> agree with me, I will know that my request to you is not futile,
> and I hope to hear from you.

C.G. Jung. Zürich. October 10, 1938.

Jung writes that he wants to go deeply into the manuscript.

> Just that you must leave me the necessary time, as with my big workload I seldom have the opportunity to read a manuscript of such scope.

Alfred Wolfsohn. Berlin—Eichenkamp. Zikadenweg 39. 28 November 1938.

In this letter Wolfsohn insists on the urgency of a discussion in relation to:

> ...the special circumstances in which I find myself, about which I do not need to explain, I make this request in an emergency as your hearing of it is of decisive significance for my further existence. Because of this urgency I ask you again to read my book, and in this way to decide if you expect my visit or not.
>
> I feel myself to be entitled to this request because the people in Berlin to whom I have given my manuscript for assessment have unanimously expressed to me the deep impression it has elicited.
>
> I am not concerned to ask for satisfaction of a personal ambition, even of the most refined kind, as my only concern is to fulfill a task that has been ordained me. I will value and honour your decision, even if it is against me. If I plead for myself, it is done out of the conviction that, more than passive readers, you need people who regard their only mission as making certain that their work falls on fertile soil.

C.G. Jung. Zürich. 8 December 1938.

> I could not read the manuscript yet as I was overburdened with work. I hope to do so soon, during my vacation, and to be able to offer you my opinion. With me, matters of such scope do need more time, since because of my practice and other obligations I am fully occupied. If you do have another urgent matter I kindly ask you to write to me.

Alfred Wolfsohn. Berlin. 8 January 1939.

Wolfsohn writes that he may be able to emigrate to England.

> As you will recall, I must strive with all my strength, to be able to have a discussion with you.

He writes that after obtaining his visa for England he can get a transit visa to travel via Switzerland.

> …as soon as I can show an invitation from that country. The eventual necessary security payment would be provided for me. In order that I may take the necessary steps, I would need a short written invitation from you.
>
> I do not know if you have already read my manuscript, and thus if you are willing to let me know your decision with regards to our discussion. I any case, in support of my request, I submit a letter from Herr Dr. Werner Engel, who has read my manuscript, which interested him greatly, and on this basis has decided to take singing lessons with me.
>
> Through this doctor I have had the opportunity to see my assertions confirmed, in the widest sense. This medical doctor, who is fully familiar with your science, came to me without a *(singing)* voice, and with no musical background. The surprisingly rapid success of my efforts were therefore possible, because the foundation for us both to work on was provided by your knowledge.
>
> The results I have come to in this case are as follows:

Alfred Wolfsohn briefly recounts the story of Socrates, who shortly before his death, was told in a dream to learn to play the flute, which he did. In contrast to the usual Jungian interpretation of Socrates' action, Wolfsohn says:

> My interpretation of the dream, from another standpoint, is that he absolutely fulfilled the meaning of the dream. It is this point of view, with all its details, which I can bring forth from my experience (*Author's note: Here Wolsohn means from his experience as a teacher*) to present to you, which would be the content of our discussion, and which in any event I know must interest you.
>
> I find it difficult to have to bother you again with my request, but I still count on your fulfilling it because I noticed that during your lecture in Berlin, you had to pause a moment when singing came up from the street outside.

This means that Alfred Wolfsohn perceived Jung as aware of the power of the voice. An accompanying letter, presumably from Dr. Engels was listed, but not included. There was no reason given by the library for its absence.

Alfred Wolfsohn. Berlin—Grunewald. 21 February 1939.

> I ask you, very politely, please briefly inform me if you are willing to support my request or not.
>
> To support my wish I can only say that under the given circumstances, it means a torture to have to wait without any kind of reply. I have already told you that I am prepared for a rejection. Because I do not know how far I can count on you, my only concern now is that the ordeals to which a person in my situation is exposed to should not be increased.

C.G. Jung. Zürich. 6 March 1939.

> Because in every respect I am over burdened with work, it is unfortunately absolutely impossible for me to do something for you. I must completely limit myself to do as much as possible for my medical colleagues and cannot go beyond these borders. Your work is most assuredly very interesting and valuable in practice, but lies beyond my set boundaries.

Jung returns the unread manuscript.

> I am so sorry, that under these circumstances it did not happen earlier. I still hoped to find the necessary time to be able to occupy myself with it. With the expression of my deepest regrets.

As the story unfolded, via Veronika's translation, I found myself aware of a sub-text developing; that of a Jew in Nazi Berlin, after the time of "Kristallnacht," writing urgent letters to a gentile in neutral Switzerland, requesting his help to be able to visit. Who was it that prevented Wolfsohn from being able to meet Jung in his hotel? He says it was people working in its management; they would not have been Jewish I guess, at that late date. Could they have refused him entry because of his Jewishness? Could it have been, I wondered, that Wolfsohn hoped to show Jung that his work was of such significance for Jung's researches, that he would be enthusiastic enough to invite him to join his circle of collaborators. I do not mean to suggest that Wolfsohn was fabricating anything. No, it is clear from other sources that he was convinced of the parallel nature of his discoveries with voice and psyche, and, as referred to in the letter of 8 January 1939, that he recognised Jung's ideas had played a seminal role in the elaboration of his practice. I, too, felt disappointment at the way Jung could be interpreted to have withdrawn behind his professional veil, even though the extent of pressure from his work may well have been such as he says.

C.G.Jung. Zürich. 3 May 1955—a letter written by Jung's secretary, Aniela Jaffé (a copy of this letter was held by Marita Günther).

> On behalf of Professor Jung I thank you very much for your very interesting correspondence.

There was no reference in the archives to what this might have been.

> Today, for the time being, I only wish to inform you, that a psychologist from Zürich, who has worked for a long time at the CG Jung Institute, and has worked analytically with Frau Professor Jung, is travelling to London soon, and is very interested in your research. Her name is Mrs. Dora M. Kalff.
>
> It would be nice if you could get in touch with her. She is musical and therefore will find the necessary understanding for your work. I hardly believe that Prof. Jung himself will be able to give attention to your research. In his old age he has to be sparing with his strength, and in general he hands such tasks over to his circle of students. So much the better that it comes about, that at this time someone of us goes to London and I will then certainly hear more about

the meeting. Frau Dr. Kalff is in London for reasons of study.

I was unable to find any reference to such a meeting having occurred, nor did any of Wolfsohn's former students whom I asked, recall it.

"The Magic Chord" in *AND*, 1971; photo Ivan Midderigh.